DES MOINES
ARCHITECTURE & DESIGN

DES MOINES
ARCHITECTURE & DESIGN

JAY PRIDMORE

WITH NEW PHOTOGRAPHY BY
STEVE FORITANO

THE
History
PRESS

Published by The History Press
Charleston, SC
www.historypress.net

Copyright © 2015 by Jay Pridmore

Front cover, top row, middle: Stained glass. *Steve Foritano*; *middle*: Senate chamber. *Jason Mrichina*; *bottom left*: Theater space. *Kerri Photography*.

First published 2015

Manufactured in the United States

ISBN 978.1.62619.975.0

Library of Congress Control Number: 2015953066

Notice: The information in this book is true and complete to the best of our knowledge. It is offered without guarantee on the part of the author or The History Press. The author and The History Press disclaim all liability in connection with the use of this book.

CONTENTS

Acknowledgements   7
Introduction   9

1. Prairie Palace in Des Moines   13
2. A Living State Capitol   22
3. Sherman Hill in the Past and Present   37
4. Commercial Design in Old Des Moines   47
5. Remembering Piety Hill   57
6. Grand Avenue and South of Grand   65
7. Des Moines' City Beautiful Movement   80
8. Tall Buildings of the Jazz Age   95
9. Des Moines Art Center: Expansive Icon   107
10. Modernism at Drake   118
11. An Urban Campus for Finance   131
12. Designing Des Moines' Future   145

Select Bibliography   167
Index   169
About the Author   175

ACKNOWLEDGEMENTS

This book took form when Tom Leslie, professor of architecture at Iowa State University, introduced me to Ben Gibson, acquisitions editor at The History Press. Tom knew of my interest in Des Moines architecture and suggested that I might be the author Ben was looking for. To both of them I am most grateful. I made contact with people whose financial assistance became indispensable in this project. John Pappajohn provided early support as well as interviews that helped me reconstruct important episodes of Des Moines history. Bill Knapp and Gerry Neugent were also generous with support, especially for the acquisition of photographs. I must also thank two acquaintances of long standing, Steve Parrish and DT Doan, whose enduring goodwill were of great assistance in enabling me to find my way in Des Moines.

In researching this book and writing the story, I was dependent on people who understand aspects of the story far better than I do. Many were extremely generous in explaining both broad strokes and fine detail of Des Moines architecture. High on this list were Cal Lewis, former partner of HLKB and now professor at Iowa State; Paul Mohr of the State Historic Preservation Office; Tim Hickman of Substance Architecture; local historian John Zeller; and Kirk Blunck of Knowles Blunck.

Quite naturally, I prevailed on many people for interviews and assistance, without which this book would not have been possible. They include Paul Mankins and Julie Severson of Substance Architecture; Jack Porter, Marty Gross, Rob McCammon, David Schlarmann, York Taenzer and Judy McClure of the Sherman Hill Association; photographer John Hallstrom, formerly of Sherman Hill; Jeff Fleming and Christine Doolittle of the Des Moines Art Center; Bart Schmidt, Maura Lyons, Claudia Frazer, Jarad Bernstein, Danny Akright and Paul Morrison of Drake University; district judge Robert Blink, who made splendid photos of the Polk County Courthouse; photographer Cameron Campbell; Bill Dikis, formerly of RDG Planning and Design and currently of Architectural Strategies; Scotney Fenton, Michelle Sacco and Cindi

Michelsen of RDG; Larry Ericsson, formerly of Wetherell Ericsson, which became part of RDG; Karen Wiede of Skidmore Owings and Merrill; professor Nick Adams of Vassar College; Allison Fegley of Hoyt Sherman Place; photographer Kerri Hays; Carey Nagel, Erin Gehle and Pilar Tromacek of BNIM; Tina Rhodes of Genesis Architectural Design; Sheila Streicher, Steve Thilges and Michele Minske of Principal Financial; author Vicki Ingham, who is a member of the Cathedral Church of St. Paul; Steve Stimmel and Tim Bungert of Brooks Borg Skiles; Scott Allen of OPN Architects; Alexander Grgurich of Nelson Construction; Percy Keck and John M.Y. Lee, formerly of the office of Edward Larrabee Barnes; Lisa Schneider of Terrace Hill; Barbara Filer, formerly of Terrace Hill; Jimmy Center of Governor Branstad's staff; photographer Bill Gentsch; Ben Weese, formerly of Harry Weese and Associates; professor Mario Gandelsonas of Agrest and Gandelsonas and of Princeton University; Caleb Buland and Shawn Foutch of Foutch Brothers LLC; Kim Klingkade of Bergman Folkers Plastic Surgery; Jason Alread, formerly of HLKB and now director of the University of Florida School of Architecture; Greg Wattier, John Bloom and Dan Drendel of Slingshot Architecture; Martin Wolf of Solomon Cordwell Buenz; Gyo Obata of HOK; Gen Obata, formerly of HOK; Keith Rollenhagan of Rollenhagen Design; Jack Bowman, formerly of the Office of Mies van der Rohe; Jessica Reinert, Amy Spike, Vicki Scott, Pamela French and Jennifer Peters of the Iowa chapter of the American Institute of Architects; Kari Tindall of Court Avenue Suites; Andrea Hauer, Jason Van Essen and Mary Neiderbach of the City of Des Moines; Diann Evans of U.S. Bank; Jennifer James, Barbara Beving Long and Patricia Eckhardt, independent architectural historian/consultants; Kimberly Broderick of the Integer Group; Rebekah Kentfield, formerly of the Integer Group; Pamela Bookey of the Temple for the Performing Arts; Rachel Lopez of BH Management; John Zickefoose, a docent at Terrace Hill and administrator of the Cathedral Church of St. Paul; Megan Sibbel, Laura Sadowsky and Amy Saylor of Salisbury House; Joan Arnett and Craig Cronbaugh of the Iowa State Capitol; photograph Ben Easter; photographer Caroline Jones; photographer and blogger Barbara Henning; photographer Douglas Steiner; Rick Pope of American Republic Insurance; David Busick, formerly of American Republic; Randy Manear formerly of Principal Financial and now Terrus Real Estate Group; Elaine Estes, formerly of the Des Moines Public Library; Niki de Phillips of Kum and Go; John McGinnis, former resident of the Coffee Mansion and author of a monograph on the subject; and former governor Robert E. Ray.

I was fortunate to have met attorney Steve Foritano, who is also a skilled photographer. Steve made new photographs for this book and provided needed advice as to the inclusion of various buildings.

The greatest good fortune in this book was the overall delight in writing it. The depth of the architecture of Des Moines and the genuine openness of the people of Des Moines brought to this project pleasures that will be hard to reproduce in the future.

INTRODUCTION

Iowans, according to persistent myth, are modest people, unwilling to call attention to themselves, ready to give credit to others. If so, it stands to reason that the characteristic would show up in its architecture. Are its buildings quiet and reposed? The Des Moines Art Center mostly is. Do architects do more with less? One thinks of the new Central Public Library. The power of restraint is a good working theory of architecture and a valid looking glass to view the long architectural history of Des Moines.

There are exceptions to the modesty theory, naturally. A big one turns out to be the city's earliest surviving building of note. One can't know directly why Benjamin Franklin Allen wanted his house, Terrace Hill, to look like it was designed for Paris, or why he used seven kinds of wood in the splendid millwork inside. Probably, he wanted to be affirmed as a man of wealth. Or perhaps he hired Chicago's leading architect at the time to design his house to prove that Iowa deserved such splendor, too.

There are many impulses behind good buildings, and the history of Des Moines architecture reveals a complexity, not to mention excellence, suitable for a city of its wealth and education. Architecture is very good at incorporating characteristics of economics, technology, psychology and even morality in building design—often with an eloquence that other ways of communicating can hardly touch.

Another early Des Moines building, the Iowa State Capitol, would hardly qualify as modest either, but there is something high-minded about it, too. One thinks of the Lamp of Sacrifice, a measure for true and honest architecture, according to John Ruskin, whose *Seven Lamps of Architecture* (1849) still serves as a guide to conscientious architects and their clients. The Capitol is easily Iowa's most elaborate building if not its most loved, and it was designed at significant financial sacrifice to honor not an individual but rather the grandeur of all Iowa.

Later, a reform-minded Des Moines city government built a new Municipal Building on the river, and that perhaps is where the conscious penchant for modesty in Des

Moines architecture began. Des Moines had altered its form of government to curtail customary corruption in city halls. Completed in 1910, the Municipal Building's exterior is "chaste," in the parlance of the day. More emphatically reform-minded is its Counting Room, an open space on the main floor where the city's business was conducted, not in smoke-filled rooms but behind counters within view of everyone. The Counting Room is also called the Grand Hall, large with a bowed ceiling and demure ornament. It is not an imposing public space, but it is a delightful one with plenty of natural light.

Perhaps modesty is not always the right word. Perhaps simplicity is more apt, which describes the best architecture of our time and maybe of any other. For example, Frank Lloyd Wright was never modest, but he tried to be simple. "It is now valiant to be simple," he wrote. "It is a spiritual thing to comprehend what simplicity means." A Wright-designed home near Des Moines, the Trier House in Johnston, attests to that.

Among Wright's peers who spent more time in Des Moines than Wright did, Eliel Saarinen and his son Eero had the same idea about simplicity. The Art Center, which Eliel Saarinen completed in 1948, remains one of the nation's more ennobling art museums; it was designed as an active rejection of imperial architecture, which was still the fashion for museums at the time. Saarinen built low rustic walls to blend beautifully with the gentle terrain of Greenwood Park. His first striking wing of the Art Center is considered modern, but it is actually timeless.

With the working hypothesis that Des Moines architecture is truly exceptional, we search for reasons. One factor is definitely the Saarinens, whose sensibility meshed beautifully with that of Des Moines. Eero Saarinen was characteristically restrained in his nine distinctly modernist buildings on the Drake campus. The buildings were unconventional at the time, but Des Moines understood and approved. A writer for the *Register* amplified the common view in writing that the buildings engendered in any Drake student an "appreciation of beauty which should entitle him to a degree in liberal arts even though he never attends a class or opens a book."

Once again, modesty is the unmistakable hallmark of another Drake buildings, the Oreon E. Scott Chapel. It is a quiet design that features natural light streaming from a skylight to a dark and sparsely furnished sanctuary. Scott Chapel remains one of the most spiritual spaces in the whole of mid-century modern architecture, and while Saarinen's ability to express himself architecturally was remarkable, John McCaw, dean of the Divinity School, deserved credit too. He told Saarinen that he wanted a plain "communion table" under the shafts of light, not an altar. An altar, he believed, would elevate the ego of the minister. Not here.

It goes without saying that Mies van der Rohe found acceptance in Des Moines. His buildings, which stand out from anything around them, have the precision and repose to which architects have always aspired. "Less is more" was the Miesian mantra. Des Moines got it. Enough said.

It wasn't just the international stars who came to enjoy the straightforwardness of Des Moines. There were local architects as well, such as the firm that began in the nineteenth century with the name Proudfoot and Bird. They were the foremost architects in the city for at least half a century because of their ability to understand architectural trends and execute them with aplomb. They weren't innovators. Their ambitions were simpler. Another local firm called Tinsley, McBroom and Higgins was more shortlived but designed one of the remarkable buildings of downtown Des Moines in 1939, the Banker's Life Building (modestly called "Corporate One" by the company now called Principal Financial). Few buildings have ever been so thoroughly integrated from its engineering to it streamlined decor.

Then there was Charles E. "Chick" Herbert of the firm that became HLKB. In 1961, he founded Charles Herbert and Associates, and within a few decades, it had put its mark on downtown Des Moines with the Des Moines Civic Center, Meredith Corporation's headquarters and many other projects. In 2001, HLKB received the American Institute of Architect's Firm Award, one of the profession's highest honors. Behind the honor was the firm's ability to collaborate. Then there was simplicity. According to Kirk Blunck (the B in HLKB), Herbert said that "one good idea was enough" for a building. Young architects, teeming with ideas, needed to hear that and believe it.

We'll see that good architecture becomes contagious. Another prophet from afar, Mario Gandelsonas was teaching at Yale when he became enchanted by Des Moines and used it as a laboratory for urban planning. He said that downtown Des Moines, which grew over time and by many hands, looked like an inspired architect designed it. Gandelsonas had many ideas, but as he got to know the city's power brokers, he pushed one—the Western Gateway Park—with such patience that he did what few planners ever do. He realized his dream.

The Gandelsonas dream inspired others, including the Central Library by English architect David Chipperfield (assisted by collaborator extraordinaire HLKB) and the Pappajohn Sculpture Park. In time, it inspired a much different but somehow related renaissance on the East Side, now East Village.

Recent news is that one of the world's most famous architects, Renzo Piano, is coming to Des Moines to build a new headquarters for Kum and Go, the gas station chain. This seemed unbelievable, that an architect who designs mostly in world capitals, and mostly cultural shrines and churches, would build an office building in Iowa. One can assume that Des Moines got Piano's attention because of the Saarinens, also because of Mies, perhaps because of the river and certainly because of Gandelsonas. Piano must also have seen the Des Moines Civic Center, sited on its rakish angle to the streets around it, making an otherwise simple box interesting.

The Kum and Go building will be characterized by "lightness, simplicity and openness," Piano said when he unveiled drawings. What makes it distinctive will be upper stories shifting at narrow angles, as have been embedded in city's street layout for more than a century and more recently in its modern architecture—such as the Civic Center and the Hub Stop on the Principal Riverwalk. Piano amplifies the angle concept somewhat, but mildly, modestly. Perhaps Piano heard another Chick Herbert slogan: "To do common things uncommonly well." It's simple advice but has served Des Moines well for a long time.

Chapter 1

PRAIRIE PALACE IN DES MOINES

Terrace Hill appears as an architectural outlier even today. It sits large and alone at the crest of a slope over Grand Avenue. Its façade is so extravagant as to seem not just antique but also exotic. One can only imagine how the people of Des Moines in 1869 saw this "prairie palace," as it was sometimes called, when it went up.

In fact, Terrace Hill was regarded as a picture of good taste by most people whose opinions mattered at the time. It reflected the latest French style, with mansard roofs, sculpted cornices and decorative molding around doors and windows, touches of the sort that wealthy Americans witnessed when they visited Paris. To Iowans who had not been to Paris but had seen Chicago's State Street, it resembled the Palmer House Hotel and Marshall Field's, which were designed with the same faux-French look.

A jaw-dropping impression was the objective of Terrace Hill's first owner, Benjamin Franklin Allen, a wealthy banker who "is credited with doing more toward developing the city of Des Moines in its early history than any other one man." This epitaph, penned for his obituary, was charitable given the legal troubles and fraud in which Allen got tangled in the last period of his life. But before his downfall, Des Moines enjoyed Allen's fantastic life vicariously. High above the Raccoon River, Terrace Hill has a ninety-foot tower. The interiors were done in seven or eight species of wood. Marble fireplaces were shipped from Italy.

Lest his private residence go unobserved, Allen staged a housewarming party and invited the press. "In the center of the dining hall stood the tables, loaded with viands the gods might envy," wrote one reporter. "The centerpiece was a pyramid of baskets of natural fruit…At the end of the table were two boned turkeys buried in port colored jellies." There was also a lemon ice statuette of George Washington.

Terrace Hill was indulgent by any measure, but more importantly, the house, which is now the Governor's Mansion, is a testament to the expansive imaginations of Iowans when the state was in its infancy. There have been some people over the years who

Terrace Hill's design was meant to cast a striking image to anyone passing its site. Its style was French Second Empire, popular in 1869 when the mansion was built. *Courtesy of Terrace Hill.*

wanted to tear the house down, preferring to erase excess from the annals of Iowa. But for its architectural bravado and sheer craftsmanship—also an emblem of important families who lived there—it remains an incalculable Des Moines landmark.

B.F. Allen was every bit as colorful a figure as stories of Terrace Hill suggest. He was born in Salem, Indiana, and orphaned as a child when his parents died of cholera within a few days of each other. In 1848, at the age of nineteen, he moved to Des Moines, where his uncle had been the first commandant of Fort Des Moines. When the uncle died, he left his substantial land claims to "Frank."

Allen prospered in Iowa, first with a general store and then with a bank when banking was not formally permitted in Iowa but tolerated as a necessity for new settlers to finance land. Allen was prudent and also lucky. In an environment in which "wildcat" banknotes were printed by some banks, Allen always kept reserves of gold specie. When the bank panic of 1857 embarrassed fast operators in Iowa—and there were many—Allen was flush with hard currency. He loaned money to many local businesses and endorsed promissory notes of others whose businesses he knew were sound. He became a director of insurance companies, railroads, banks and the gas company.

WILLIAM BOYINGTON: ARCHITECT

By the end of the Civil War, Allen had become a larger-than-life character and required a larger-than-life homestead. For Terrace Hill, he purchased thirty acres about a mile west of the city, and he sent for the most distinguished architect available. That would be William W. Boyington of Chicago with whom he chose the French Second Empire style, developed for the massive urban improvements that Emperor Napoleon III had recently executed in Paris.

Boyington was arguably the most accomplished architect in the West. Born in Massachusetts, he began his career as a carpenter and developed a taste for the shapes and textures that could be wrought of wood. He then moved to New York, where he worked for an architect and engineer. He returned to Massachusetts to serve in the legislature where he chaired the Committee on Public Buildings. By the 1850s, while still in his thirties, he moved to Chicago, perceiving opportunity in a city that was growing as very few cities had grown before.

In Chicago architectural history, Boyington might be considered Old Testament in the sense that his career flourished before the Great Chicago Fire, after which came innovations that led directly to skyscrapers. Boyington's eye was for tradition and precedent, and he skillfully adapted old styles for current uses. This made him a sought-after architect in Chicago mostly for large-scale buildings. His most famous

The Second Empire style was formal but had the practical advantage of asymmetry. *Courtesy of Library of Congress Prints and Photographs Division.*

work became the Chicago Water Tower, a Gothic Revival design best known as a survivor of the Great Fire.

While architects in Chicago and Des Moines worked from pattern books with pictures of buildings that could be copied, Boyington traveled several times to Europe, once with a client who was building an opera house in Chicago. He also came to understand that the Second Empire style had useful characteristics aside from its association with France. Because it was developed to line the irregular streets of Paris, it was asymmetrical. Because uniformity was enforced on street after street, it had a certain repetition that was a practical advantage.

Terrace Hill is commonly regarded as one of America's prime examples of Second Empire design. Among its marks are the beveled quoins on the corners of the brick walls and the colorful patterns in the slate tiles of the roof. The imposing central tower in front is balanced with smaller ones to the sides, and a preponderance of arches in doors and windows of the façade has a unifying effect on the whole. Details appear ornate and complex, but they were wrought with a sense of geometry that renders a striking profile a century and a half later.

Boyington's love of craftsmanship comes through in the interior as well. To call it modern would be overstating the case, but it has an openness and "organic" quality—with abundant sunlight and natural materials—that would mark the most advanced and even "modern" architecture for decades to come. In the grand hall of the first floor, many varied types of wood give paneling, cornices and scrollwork a chromatic dimension. The stairway represents a masterpiece of Des Moines carpenters. Less obvious (and now largely carpeted) are parquet floors, which directed the eye in different directions, as in the case of the narrow boards forming a cross in the central hall's midsection. It subtly reinforces the sense of interlocking spaces of the main floor. The spatial flow from room to room does anticipate interiors designed by later architects such as Frank Lloyd Wright.

Saving Terrace Hill

Poor Allen could enjoy his splendid house for only five years. By 1874, he had moved to Chicago, where he had bought a bank. It appeared he was moving for an opportunity that he could not pass up. What was soon revealed was that his acquisition, the Cook County Bank, was meant to prop up his financial house of cards. It did not work out—the bank panic of 1873 would last six years—and his property was systematically liquidated.

Allen's asset that he was most reluctant to lose was Terrace Hill. As his bankruptcy was administered by the courts, he attempted to prove that he had retained Iowa residency, thus enabling him to keep his residence. It was a weak case, as he had been living in Chicago. He also attempted to put the house in the hands of an educational institution and then a hospital—neither plan worked out. As he clearly loved Terrace Hill, its eventual fate was probably the best he could ask for. It was purchased in 1884 by Frederick Marion Hubbell, another of Des Moines' oligarchs, though a more temperate and solvent one.

Hubbell was one of the true fathers of modern Iowa. He did not start with the nest egg that Allen had. Instead, as a very young man, he got a job in a land office, where he kept his eye peeled for nicely priced real estate. He found it. In the 1850s, Hubbell was buying county tax warrants at below-par prices. He paid delinquent taxes on the properties, which he then sold and bought more warrants. "I think that is trading pretty well," he wrote in his diary. He also chose his partners well, going into law practice with Jefferson S. Polk, getting into railroads and investing in the insurance business with Allen, among others.

As Allen's protracted bankruptcy was being settled, Hubbell (partnered with Polk) got Terrace Hill and most of the land around it for $60,000. As for his motivations, it's likely that he was more interested in "trading well" than a palatial lifestyle, and the transaction was profitable. Shortly after the purchase, Hubbell and Polk engaged an English landscape designer to subdivide twenty-two of Terrace Hill's original thirty acres and created a neighborhood, Polk-Hubbell Park, the following year.

As far as moving into the big house, Hubbell seems to have delighted in the house once he got there. He did extensive remodeling. The stencils on walls and ceilings as seen today were originally Hubbell's. New furniture, some of it modern at the time, was also introduced around the turn of the century. Bookcases in the library and a built-in breakfront in the dining room are examples of the Arts and Crafts style that was seeping into interior design at the time. A massive stained-glass window at

The grand staircase of Terrace Hill was part of B.F. Allen's original design. The stenciling was added by the Hubbell family after 1884 in the elaborate style fashionable at that moment in time. *Caroline Jones photograph.*

The library has high Victorian furniture along with later, simpler bookcases. *Caroline Jones photograph.*

the landing of the staircase may have been the Hubbells' most imposing mark, though restoration architect William Wagner (who worked here in the 1970s) believed that it existed prior to Hubbell. In any case, it gave an especially noble air to the house, which Hubbell grew accustomed to, especially at social affairs such as the wedding of his daughter Beulah to a Swedish count.

THE GOVERNOR'S MANSION

Another sign of Hubbell's character, if not his affection for his house, was the ironclad trust that he created in his lifetime, designed to keep his property intact until, it was said, the year 2000. The house did not make it that far, but Terrace Hill stayed in the family until 1971, when the last of his sons died and the trustees donated the mansion, outbuildings and remaining acres to the state. The intention was to make it the residence of the governor of Iowa.

This was early in the preservation movement, and the process of restoring the house was not just arduous, but it also nearly collapsed in the face of politics. Terrace Hill's renovation, even after work was begun under Republican governor Robert E. Ray, encountered opposition. First off, the third-floor ballroom was converted into an apartment for the governor. But then in 1973, the legislature turned down a request for $450,000 to restore the rest of the house. A waste of money, said some legislators, and one even proposed that the governor and his family be evicted and given $800 a month to move elsewhere.

The Rays stayed put, but the issue remained. Later, a Democrat running for governor promised that if elected, he would not live in such a white elephant. Playing the "Terrace Hill card" didn't work, and the candidate lost, but it wasn't just the politicians who were discouraging. Even the architectural profession disparaged it. Architect Larry Ericsson, a partner (along with Wagner) at the firm of Marquardt and Wetherell, which was doing the restoration, got little support from colleagues. "Even our peers looked at my firm with a jaundiced eye," Ericsson said. "They treated us as the guys who just did old stuff."

Not to be defeated, supporters of the project created a not-for-profit Terrace Hill Society and took on responsibility for the restoration. They came up with the idea of minting a Terrace Hill Preservation Medallion, selling copies to the public to raise funds. It was a great success and proved that old buildings are something that the public appreciates. By 1978, even the crustiest legislators were exhausted by the fight. "It's been a fiasco, but we've got it," said one old pol referring to Terrace Hill. "We might as well finish it."

The physical work of restoring stencils and woodwork, as well as recarving and recasting cornices outside, was a long process that showed architects that patience is a key virtue in preservation. By 1981, $3.5 million had been spent on the project. It is a popular tourist destination now. Both political parties have had governors occupy it. And as all buildings require sometimes expensive maintenance, the politicians have moved to other issues, and Terrace Hill stands as a true symbol of the state, its ambition and its majesty.

Opposite: Terrace Hill originally sat on thirty acres. Today the grounds are reduced but include the stable, which is now a tour center. *Courtesy of Terrace Hill.*

Chapter 2

A LIVING STATE CAPITOL

Today's Iowa State Capitol, completed in 1886, is nothing like the previous one, except they both have domes, almost (not entirely) mandatory in American statehouses since time immemorial. The Old Capitol in Iowa City is simple, almost rustic, and feels like it has ghosts haunting it. The new Capitol—rather, the one now occupied by state government—looks like an antique, but almost anyone who knows the building would acknowledge it as a symbol of Iowa's present as well as its past.

The Capitol, on the East Side's highest point, still represents ambitions that reach back to a time when the new state was asserting its identity. Its domes, five of them, can be seen for miles across the prairie. Its permanence reflects the democracy that would buoy the state through thick and thin. One could say that its baroque ornament symbolizes the complexity of the government's mission, and while aspects of the building may violate our modern taste for simplicity, few would deny that Iowa's Capitol is something to be proud of.

This story began for Des Moines in 1855 when the state constitutional convention voted to move the capital city closer to the middle of Iowa. Fair-minded delegates sought a place near the absolute geographic center of the state, and they settled on the confluence of two rivers, the Des Moines and Raccoon. Reaching consensus on the subject came largely because putting the capital in Des Moines politically benefited almost no one. It had an abandoned fort, a few dry goods stores and quite a few taverns. It had recently suffered a devastating flood, leaving a clear slate, which perhaps also appealed to the delegates.

Most local settlers were fine with the choice—they included B.F. Allen and Frederick Hubbell at early points in their careers who may have been too savvy to insist on having the Capitol building sited near land they owned. Instead, it went to the East Side when two landowners agreed to donate the site. Hopeful that so much government activity would trigger a buildup in land prices, one of the donors, Willson Alexander Scott,

The Capitol was built to occupy a high point on the city's East Side. *Courtesy of Iowa Legislative Information Office.*

even paid to have a first temporary building constructed. That was the so-called Brick Capitol, just a few yards downslope from the present one. Scott's hopes did not work out, as he went into debt on that deal and had to leave Des Moines to seek a fortune and repay it. He died before succeeding, making his the first frustration on which the monument of the State Capitol was eventually built.

FIGHTING FOR A STATELY CAPITOL

The architecture of the permanent building was not particularly controversial, though political hurdles seemed like they were everywhere. "Our people were too generally educated and intelligent not to desire something worthy of admiration, something expressing the dignity and higher aspirations of the State," wrote John A. Kasson, a member of the state House of Representatives at the time. Yet, in his article entitled "The Fight for the New Capitol," written in 1900, Kasson also recounted the ironies:

"The splendid architecture of the Greeks was decreed by people occupying a much smaller territory than Iowa." But in Des Moines, decreeing anything was a struggle. "If the Macedonians and Thracians had been called upon to vote a great building in Athens by the aid of their taxes, it would have been voted down," he wrote.

A series of difficult roll calls was required to start and continue construction. In one political flare-up, legislators from Clinton County attempted in 1867 to stall the project until a proper railroad connection could be built to enable use of their local stone on the building. Less focused opponents included "our old and irreconcilable enemies," wrote Kasson, including one who "far more loved to attack than defend any cause." Entertaining shenanigans were devised, too. On the night before one critical vote, a pro-Capitol legislator "had been beset by some anti-Capitol members [who] drugged him with whisky." Allies lobbied him with coffee. By 1872, construction had begun when an allocation bill was passed with an amendment "instructing the commission to keep in view a cost of $1,500,000." The words "to keep in view" seemed to some like a blank check. If it was, it was postdated.

Despite politics, the niceties of architecture were important to the civic spirit, not to mention Iowans' competitive pride. Iowa was joining a flurry of capitol-building activity after the Civil War, in part because the nation was in need of strong political symbols to counteract the terrible war's trauma. Building was also driven by increased patronage in state governments, as this was the Gilded Age of great wealth and intractable pirates. State capitols also became coveted commissions for leading architects such as Richard Morris Hunt, H.H. Richardson and McKim, Mead and White, all of whom designed state capitols.

Architecture would evolve and change in this period, but most agreed that the Neoclassical style was appropriate for American democracy. This reached back to Jefferson, who had modeled the Virginia State Capitol on the temples of Greece. Construction of the Renaissance-style dome of the U.S. Capitol continued even during the Civil War, as President Lincoln believed "it is a sign we intend the Union shall go on." It did, and in the next few years, states flush with money or swelling with Manifest Destiny were eager to have equally proud buildings.

The Iowa Capitol was designed in a period when the "modern" preference was for a Neoclassical variant, the French Second Empire style, which also inspired Terrace Hill. National discussion surrounded this style in the 1870s and '80s, and a leading East Coast architect, G.J.F. Bryant, explained that choice for his New Hampshire statehouse design: "It will be at once recognized, by all those conversant with such matters as the prevailing style of modern Europe...I have earnestly desired in this respect, not to fall behind the progress of art." Besides admiration of France, American architects were searching for an "American" style. The searching was "by addition" and led to ornamental flourishes that could make the French seem staid.

When the legislature called for proposals from qualified architects, it advertised the competition in publications nationwide. Four finalists were considered by members of Iowa's appointed Capitol Commission, which was consulted by Edward Clark, then architect of the U.S. Capitol in Washington. Clark's opinion turned out to be decisive. He preferred the scheme from the office of Chicago architect John Cochrane, who had also recently won the commission for the capitol building for Illinois.

In fact, Cochrane was probably not the primary designer for either Illinois or Iowa. Rather, credit goes to Alfred H. Piquenard, a Frenchman with a background as ornate as his building. Piquenard had been born near Paris but had become a devotee of the Icanrians, a semi-religious sect that professed socialism. With the ascension of Emperor Napoleon III, many Icanrians left for America and settled in Nauvoo, Illinois, recently vacated by the Mormons. From there, Piquenard made it to the architectural profession and to Chicago.

Piquenard's antipathy for Napoleon III did not mean that he rejected the emperor's architecture. Understanding its popularity in America, Piquenard mastered the Second Empire repertoire and more. His Iowa Capitol features towers, mansards and pediments, with Greek porticoes on four sides. A primary dome over the central primary dome over the rotunda was a predictable design for a state capitol. More adventurous design-wise were towers on the four corners, perhaps drawn from the

The architect of the Capitol was the Frenchman A.H. Piquenard, and he designed it in a manner distinctly reminiscent of the French Second Empire. *Courtesy of Special Collections, Cowles Library, Drake University.*

Louvre in Paris, with those towers capped by smaller domes. Another distinct feature is that the Capitol is multichromatic—not pure white—in the short-lived fashion of its time. It is a reposed design but not reticent. Critic Henry-Russell Hitchcock (leading arbiter of modern architecture) wrote in 1976 that the Iowa Capitol seems to "grow from the land," though with "a cosmopolitan touch befitting a maturing state."

A DESIGN DECADES IN THE MAKING

The Capitol is a fine work of architecture, but if the design appears overly complex, that may be because there was nothing simple about building it. Complexity began with the design competition, which the Piquenard scheme won, but in which the interior of another entrant, Iowa architect J.J. Farrand, was judged by the jury to be superior. No one documented how the latter architect influenced the ultimate design of spaces within, but one can assume that discussions on the subject were not muted.

In 1871, the cornerstone was laid and foundation built with limestone from Rock Creek in Van Buren County. Political considerations led to that choice of building material, but whatever the considerations were, Rock Creek limestone was the wrong choice. The stone was infused with moisture, or "quarry sap," as it was called, and very shortly after the foundation was set, it cracked and had to be removed. A more successful stone for the foundation was found elsewhere in Iowa, but construction was once again delayed.

Other things beset the project along the way. By 1872, Cochrane left the project, as he believed there was more lucrative work to be had in Chicago in the wake of the Great Fire. Cochrane's departure did not greatly change the design, but more setbacks occurred when Piquenard died in 1876. He was replaced by Mifflin E. Bell of the Piquenard office. Happily, Bell resisted what might have been fatal, which would have been to assert his own signature by adding more ornament. The main contribution of Bell, later architect of the United States Interior Department, appears to have been to adjust the proportions of the main dome and reduce its complexity, if only slightly.

When the Capitol was dedicated in 1884, much of the interior decoration was left unfinished. But the legislative chambers were completed, and a flamboyant blend of Egyptian and classical motifs is particularly evident in the Senate. What we see in the House of Representatives chamber is noticeably more restrained, but only because the original, which resembled the Senate, was gutted by a fire in 1904 (caused by workers converting from gas to electric light) and replaced by the simpler style in fashion at that time.

Above: The Senate Chamber in the early 1900s. *Courtesy of Special Collections, Cowles Library, Drake University.*

Below: The Iowa House of Representatives appears somewhat simpler than other parts of the Capitol's interior, as it was remodeled around 1904 in more subdued times. *Courtesy of Iowa Legislative Information Office.*

Artwork for the Capitol's interior was commissioned to the finest sculptors and painters from around the nation. *Courtesy of Iowa Legislative Information Office*

Opposite: The five-story atrium space of the Capitol's law library is still used for research. The marvels of its design have survived changes in taste and even a near-disastrous fire. *Courtesy of Iowa Legislative Information Office*

In the manner of its time, the rotunda reflects the Gilded Age taste for luxury. *Courtesy of Iowa Legislative Information Office.*

Opposite, top: In the 1880s and '90s, when the rotunda was completed, decorative painting and stenciling reached heights considered suitable for Iowa's shrine of democracy. *Courtesy of Iowa Legislative Information Office.*

Opposite, bottom: *Westward* by Edwin Blashfield of Philadelphia is the Capitol's most direct symbol of Iowa's pride in its frontier roots. *Courtesy of Iowa Legislative Information Office.*

Decorating the rest of the interior, including the rotunda, which reaches to the top of the dome, came mostly in the first decade of the new century, and despite money-caused delays, the commissioners sought the most distinguished artists available to paint the walls, mosaic the floors and sculpt the statuary. As reported in the press at the time, Iowa followed the custom of other state capitols, which was to employ artists of "well established reputation, known to be capable of the best work, and to give [them] carte blanche to work out the designs for the entire decoration."

The most conspicuous work of art in the buildings is the romantic mural *Westward* on the main landing of the central stairway. It artist, Edwin Blashfield of Philadelphia, had done murals in other state capitols and painted the dome

in the reading room of the Library of Congress. There is nothing reticent about *Westward*, which is forty feet wide, with handsome pioneers riding from right to left in a covered wagon. Angelic messengers float down from the sky. Disembodied faces appear from behind stalks of corn to the left (west) to symbolize Iowans of the future. Its meaning is unmistakable, as was Iowa's optimistic view of its destiny.

A Twenty-Year Restoration

In retrospect, no one can be quite sure why the original commissioners decided to buy sandstone from Carroll County, Missouri, for the elaborate and ubiquitous exterior trim. Perhaps there were no politics involved, and it was selected because it was softer than other stone and could be carved easily. Unfortunately, soft sandstone also meant that deterioration was a risk, which began as early as 1904, when a commissioners' report noted that something like acid rain was taking a toll on carved ornament.

As time passed, the problem got increasingly hard to ignore. By the 1970s, deterioration was extreme, with much of the carved stone eroded to a faceless surface. From a distance, the Capitol was still stately and impressive. Up close, it was even dangerous. "Rosettes were falling off from the underside of soffits," remembered Bill Dikis, then a partner with the firm Bussard Dikis of Des Moines. Dikis had been active on the committee for architectural restoration of the American Institute of Architects. In 1981, a member of the Capitol Commission at the time asked him to have a look at the problem.

Neither Dikis nor the politicians involved were heedless of the immensity of a proper restoration job. Dikis and his firm, which later became Renaissance Design Group, also quickly discerned that sufficient funds for the project could be allocated from the state budget only slowly if at all, and they sketched out an eleven-phase plan costing some $18 million. Ultimately, the project continued for more than twenty years and cost $125 million. Some years, work was slowed due to the dismal economy resulting from the farm crisis. "Some years, all we could do was buy the stone, then carve it the next year," said Scotney Fenton, a lead architect at RDG and who stayed on the project until it was substantially complete in 2001.

Beyond mere money, the process challenged the skills of scores of design professionals and craftspeople. Architects produced drawings of sections of cornice or other ornament and sent them to stone suppliers in Indiana, where carvers dressed the durable Bedford stone. Ornamental painters seemed always to be somewhere on scaffolding overhead, even in offices where state work was otherwise being done. Metalworkers used molds based on surviving chandeliers to produce decorative bronze fixtures like those that were originally illuminated with gas.

"It's not a building built to economy," admitted Tim Moraine of the Iowa State Historical Society. But practicality is never far from the surface. The gold leafing of the dome, for example, must have seemed extravagant in 1883 when originally applied, as it did in 1999 when the materials alone to regild the dome cost $160,000. But when such work is done, it lasts thirty years or more, as opposed to a mere paint job, which might fade in a year. "So it really is more economical to cover the dome with gold," said Joan Arnett, supervisor of the Capitol tour guides, who adds, "You have to admit it is very striking."

A WORTHY NEIGHBOR: THE STATE HISTORICAL BUILDING

Tastes would change as the nineteenth century progressed, and they turned sharply away from the baroque flourishes of the State Capitol within just a few years of its dedication. Architecture at the most prestigious levels moved to a more classical whiteness, such as characterized the U.S. Capitol decades before, and which was so striking in Chicago at the World's Columbian Exposition in 1893. It inspired the refined Neoclassicism of the State Historical, Memorial and Art Building (now the Ola Babcock Miller Building, which houses the Iowa State Library), the first part of which was completed in 1899.

The reasons for changes in taste are almost always subjective. In this case, the trend was associated with Washington and Chicago, as well as the famous new building for the Boston Public Library, which so consciously resembled something from the Italian Renaissance. Wealth and confidence at the turn of the century justified such a building in Iowa as well.

By 1897, land for a historical museum was assembled north of the Capitol, and the architectural firm was selected: Smith and Gutterson, which would also soon work on the Des Moines Public Library. Oliver Smith was a favorite of officials in the city and state, largely because of his entrepreneurial skills. While no great designer himself, he partnered over the course of his career with a series of talented architects such as Frank Gutterson, a Minnesotan who studied the Neoclassical Beaux-Arts technique at the Massachusetts Institute of Technology.

The inherent symmetry of the Beaux-Arts style enabled the state to do what was economically necessary, which was to build only one wing in 1899. It stood easily alone, small but stately, for eleven years. Happily, interest in this building on the part of the legislature did not wane, partly because of wide admiration

The Ola Babcock Miller Building, which once housed the state museum, now serves as the State Library of Iowa. *Wetteland photograph. Courtesy of State Library of Iowa.*

The State Historical Memorial went up in sections. This west wing stood comfortably by itself for more than a decade before the central and west wings were completed. *Vintage photograph courtesy of John McGinnis.*

for Charles Aldrich, the original curator of the museum that would occupy it. Aldrich was a naturalist and collector, as well as being a former legislator himself, and had the support of his ex-colleagues in the statehouse. By 1910, the central and eastern sections of the building were completed in the accepted style and appeared very much a single piece.

As for the details, Aldrich quite likely lobbied that it should be built of limestone from Le Grand, Iowa. Aldrich wrote that it was only right to choose Iowa stone, and in fact, he knew Le Grand stone for its beauty and durability and also for the rich fossil deposits of that locale. This Iowa limestone appears to be the equal in quality of that of Indiana, though Le Grand could not produce the quantities that made Bedford, Indiana, almost synonymous with public architecture in Des Moines in decades to come.

What is clear from the Historical Building is that Iowa state officials cared about architecture and understood it. The original interior flowed from gallery to gallery, and exhibits were designed "on a scale of equal magnitude and artistic skill with that which has become so acceptable in the State Capitol," as a state publication of the time pointed out. Economy was inherent in false finishes in place

The State Historical Memorial and Art Building went up over a period of more than a decade but was designed with a simple consistency that makes it appear as if it was built in a single piece. *Courtesy of Special Collections, Cowles Library, Drake University.*

The Historical Building was dedicated to the state's desire to celebrate its past and its culture. *Courtesy of Special Collections, Cowles Library, Drake University.*

of true marble columns. But art graced the galleries, with portrait busts specially commissioned and large allegorical canvasses moved from other buildings of state government. Its architecture achieved, and still achieves, its calling, which in this case was to transcend the budgets, politics and bureaucracy to project an image of Iowa that everyone could share.

Chapter 3

SHERMAN HILL IN THE PAST AND PRESENT

In the 1880s, the neighborhood that would be called Sherman Hill was desirable for its position high above downtown Des Moines and upwind of the factories that produced prodigious quantities of smoke. Its prestige was spurred by the first stately building in the neighborhood, Hoyt Sherman's house, which was built in 1877 on what is now Woodland Avenue. But like any neighborhood of its age, it has had its ups and downs.

At the turn of the last century, Sherman Hill remained an enclave for the early business elite, Des Moines' bankers and industrialists. By the Depression, the neighborhood was in decline, and after World War II, it was downright dangerous. Fortuitously, urban renewal left Sherman Hill untouched while leveling so many other historic areas. That enabled the neighborhood to be rediscovered by rehabbers in the 1970s and later made a landmark district. Young professionals found its Victorian architecture an antidote to suburban tract houses. Families moved in and restored unique homes with broad front porches. Those porches, among other elements, engendered a community that made Sherman Hill a model of historic preservation.

"Sherman Hill" is a latter-day name borrowed from Hoyt Sherman, a leading early banker in Iowa and brother of Civil War general William Tecumseh Sherman. Sherman's architect is unknown, though architects with an eye for history have speculated that the place might have been the work of William Foster, Des Moines' leading architect at the time and one of its only trained ones. The style was a mix, including a tall central tower with a French Second Empire profile, not unlike the tower over the front door of B.F. Allen's house, Terrace Hill.

Houses were conscious symbols of success in the Gilded Age in America, a period of wealth accumulation when a family home projected an air of permanence to a fortune that might in reality be fragile. Banking, Sherman's and Allen's métier, was hardly the stable occupation at the time that it would later become. Both men faced risks that included the hazards of wildcat currency, disastrous floods and economic crashes.

There was also rivalry. In the rough and tumble of Des Moines finance, Sherman and Allen were among partners of the Equitable Life Insurance Company of Iowa, but there was little sense that they were staunch business allies. When Allen's finances collapsed, it was another Equitable partner, Jefferson Polk, who became Allen's most aggressive creditor. "A 'Darwinian' struggle to determine the most fit, or, in some cases, the most fortuitous, may aptly describe Des Moines during this period," wrote historian William M. Ferraro of early Des Moines in 1998 in *The Annals of Iowa*. It makes sense to look at the fine homes of early businessmen through the lens of this competitive arena.

That Hoyt Sherman's house was designed by Foster is an assumption based on its similarity to another Foster house for Wesley Redhead, another early Iowan whose interests ranged from coal to insurance. Sherman's house on the West Side and Redhead's on the East were hard to miss; both had gables across the imposing façade in the Italianate manner, a kind of casual classicism. They had wood-carved ornament that helped define "Carpenter's Gothic." The Second Empire towers of both Sherman and Redhead was a feature already known locally from Terrace Hill. To a purist's eye, the Sherman house appeared a concoction of an architect who could not decide on a single style. But it was well proportioned and represented the custom, even conviction, that truly American houses should blend many styles in unique ways.

Hoyt Sherman Place, now a community center, has lost its tower but over the years added new wings for art and performance. *Courtesy of Hoyt Sherman Place.*

Hoyt Sherman Place, as it is now called, has been enlarged over the years and altered in still other styles that were popular when the work was done, and a similar mix characterizes the neighborhood that grew up around it north and west of the big house, and now Sherman Hill. To our eye, there is a certain sameness to much of it. We call it "Victorian"—mostly wood, some brick, often ornate and built largely before the turn of the last century. A closer look reveals that Sherman Hill architecture represents a continuum of change in house architecture, reflecting trends in taste and the lives of the people who lived in them.

THE MAISH HOUSE ON CENTER STREET

Among the finer houses on Sherman Hill is one of the earlier ones, built by George Maish on Center Street in 1881. Maish may have been more typical of Des Moines entrepreneurs at the time than Sherman and Allen. His idea of a home, hardly modest, was less conspicuous, with a hipped roof, carved brackets under eaves and columns holding up a wraparound porch. Each feature seems uncrowded and with classical touches. It is a house that seems even today to weather the storms of fashion as easily as the owner weathered ups and downs in business.

Maish had come to Iowa in 1869 from Pennsylvania, where he had risen modestly up the economic ladder from hardware clerk to bank teller. But he was eager for bigger opportunities, and shortly after settling in Des Moines he became owner of a drug concern called Weaver and Maish. "His geniality, cordiality and reliability not only gained for him a host of friends, but also constituted a strong attribute in his business career," according to a history of the city in 1911. He and Weaver, his brother-in-law, were challenged along the way when a rival accused them of using unauthorized alcoholic spirits in their products. Maish survived that dust-up and later got into banking.

His house was designed toward the beginning of the Gilded Age when the Italianate style represented a conservative approach to the architecture of prosperity. Maish was wealthy but not so much that he would flaunt his success. The most expensive element of the exterior was the fine porch. Then, as now, porches pointed to the importance of neighbors, a quality reflected in another remarkable characteristic of this neighborhood. The Maish House is one of five on Center Street each set progressively deeper on its lot to afford its next-door neighbor to the west a clear view of the distant State Capitol.

More lavish than the exterior, perhaps, was the Maish interior, which still contains fine woodwork: carved balusters and newel posts, doors and door frames and built-in cabinetry, intricately profiled in what is now called the Eastlake style. Eastlake

The Maish House was a stately Italianate home built in the early 1880s and became one of the neighborhood's many lovingly preserved homes in the late twentieth century. *John Hallstrom photograph. Courtesy of the photographer.*

describes an American design movement inspired by English writers like John Ruskin and William Morris, who praised medieval handcrafts for their beauty and moral uplift as an antidote to industry. Eastlake could be so intricately wrought that it was easily impressive and, ironically, turned out in factories by mass production.

REIGN OF THE QUEEN ANNE

As the neighborhood filled up with houses, large Italianates were overtaken by the Queen Anne style, a general term that points to a more complex overall design. Window treatments, porches, rooflines and other exterior features became increasingly elaborate as the 1880s progressed. As for the name, "Queen Anne" is something of a misnomer. In England it describes a period when the Stuart queen reigned in the 1700s and when Neoclassical architecture became increasingly ornamented, also called "English baroque." In America, later architecture influenced by the Gothic

Revival and decorated with ornate flourishes also, somewhat mistakenly, took the name of Queen Anne.

As a practical matter, the dozens of Queen Anne–influenced houses on Sherman Hill have a vertical profile that suited a neighborhood subdivided into small lots. An example would be the Sheuerman House at Sixteenth and Woodland on a raised site and with a tower dominating the façade. Built in 1884 for the family of Leopold Sheuerman, an owner of Capital City Woolen Mills, it was a house suitable for a family of high rank. Its roofline includes intersecting gables and an elaborate dormer, definite Queen Anne traits. More specifically, the Sheuerman House represents *early* Queen Anne, also called the "Stick style." The moniker indicates that the designer, who was perhaps a carpenter, amplified the intricacy of his work by highlighting its complex framework with elaborate carpentry and paint. "Carpenter's Gothic" also describes this house and the idea of design that valued originality and not convention.

A cheerful, if not typical, example of Queen Anne on Sherman Hill is found in the four houses on a short lane called Bridal Row on the eastern edge of the neighborhood.

Preservationists have given the Sheuerman House attention since the 1980s when the tower was rebuilt. *John Hallstrom photograph. Courtesy of the photographer.*

In 1885, Hoyt Sherman and his family subdivided this portion of the family's property on Fifteenth Street. The Shermans built these smallish houses, initially rented to newlyweds, stylishly despite their small scale. "Jerkin head" (or clipped front) gables were a new touch for Des Moines Queen Annes at the time, likely drawn from English cottages. "Eyebrow" windows, another subtle touch, are low elliptical dormers that were familiar from thatched roof cottages, also from England.

As with most houses on Sherman Hill, the architect or designer of the Bridal Row cottages is uncertain, but architect-historian Jack Porter, who lives on Sherman Hill, suggests that they may be the work of Benjamin J. Bartlett, who has at least one very similar house in the neighborhood. Bartlett was an ambitious and skilled designer of Gothic churches and public buildings, as well as homes with Queen Anne–style flourishes. Like many architects, he traveled to where he found larger and more desirable work. From Des Moines he moved to Little Rock, primarily because he won a commission for the Arkansas School for the Blind. If Bartlett's Queen Anne architecture had a complexity to it, so did his life, which included a jail term for forgery of a signature on a bond.

Return of Simplicity

Like other human endeavors, architecture changes with time, and the freestyle flourishes of Victorian homes reached their limit around 1893. That was when a national economic depression hit and put the brakes on building of all kinds. When

In 1905, the Leon Strauss family had wealth to build on Sherman Hill and the restraint to build simply in what is now called the American Foursquare style. It was restored by Jack Porter and Martha Green in what was a dangerous neighborhood in the 1970s and is now a garden district of Des Moines. *Steve Foritano photograph.*

hard times lifted four years later, it was natural that simpler designs should prevail. In some places they were influenced by the Prairie School, though the approach made famous by Frank Lloyd Wright usually required larger lots than are common on Sherman Hill. The neighborhood has a Prairie variant called "Craftsman style," cottages variously marked by straight-sawn woodwork, exposed rafter tails and shingle cladding on walls. Related and more basic still was the so-called American Foursquare. It sounds simple, and it was: a square footprint, two full stories, with a hipped roof and central dormer facing front. It was so unembellished that the standard plan could be copied from magazines and then easily altered without changing the layout.

The American Foursquare was simple but not poor. An excellent example on Sherman Hill is the house built by downtown merchant Benjamin Strauss on Eighteenth Street. It is tidy and unprepossessing outside, but inside it has marks of true Prairie School houses: fine leaded-glass windows and quarter-sawn cabinetry, mantelpieces and plate rails. A taste for handcrafts is obvious in the Strauss house, built in 1905. But Victorian frippery is over. Now owned by Jack Porter, the house has an open interior and horizontal decor, not too different from what we associate with Frank Lloyd Wright but here designed, probably without architect supervision, by fashion-conscious carpenters, builders and clients.

Model of Preservation

The diversity of styles on Sherman Hill is not particularly evident today. In its preserved state, it looks like it reaches back to a stable time of tree-lined streets little touched by change. A closer look at the architecture belies this, of course. Also mostly forgotten are the political battles that accompanied Sherman Hill's development. As early as 1878, opposition rose when an investor from Upstate New York, Tallmadge E. Brown, purchased a portion of the area and platted it with small eight-thousand-square-foot lots. Also unremembered is the anger caused when developers induced the city to close the part of Cottage Grove Avenue that once went through.

Sherman Hill seemed to reflect the laissez faire business climate at the time. In 1912, the city engineer was referring in part to Sherman Hill when he lamented, "The city of Des Moines grew so fast that the various tracts of land were laid out and accepted by the city without much regard to uniformity and as the result the map of Des Moines looks like a crazy quilt patchwork." But what seemed undemocratic then became an asset later. Sherman Hill became a cohesive community because it was tightly woven on smaller lots and also because Cottage Grove did not divide it in half.

Much later, Sherman Hill became a model of historic preservation, less as a social movement in its early stages and more through examples of pioneering individualism. In fact, both impulses would describe Ralph and Marty Gross, who first moved here in 1971 when they rented an apartment from an elderly spinster who owned several houses in the area. The landlady was no rehabber, but she was fussy about who she rented to, even though the streets were rough and even dangerous. The Grosses qualified.

"At the time, I did not know that prostitutes walked the streets," Marty said. But she learned about the rougher sides of life as a resident of Sherman Hill. She witnessed drug use and random crime, which she never saw growing up in West Des Moines. But the newlywed Grosses had been dispirited by suburban life and began to feel at home especially as they found other pioneers who had moved in too. A couple of years later they bought the Maish House, which was a wreck, but Ralph harbored the dream of occupying the place with an experimental school.

More or less to survive, the Grosses became expert at various aspects of preservation, such as repairing concrete footings beneath the once-fine wraparound porch. They began to learn the niceties of fancy carpentry, such as *kerfing*, which is the process of bending wood, in this case for fascia that curved around the perimeter of the house. They scraped decades of paint to find original colors and then found two shades of yellow for clapboards and trim after the chips were sent away for analysis. The school they imagined did not come true, but their house became a showplace.

The other part of historic preservation, the Grosses learned, was less architectural and more social. Later in the 1970s, Mayor Richard Olson had noticed the Grosses and other families staking their claim in Sherman Hill and asked Ralph to attend an urban preservation conference in Minneapolis. Gross came back with the message that critical mass in preservation required political will. That induced neighbors to form what they called the Sherman Hill Association in 1976. City hall, the police and the press took notice. Residents next got recognition by the National Register of Historic Places, and the practical consequence of that was federal tax credits for multiunit restorations. More generally, the neighbors faced the opponents of preservation together.

As another example of Sherman Hill's ups and downs, the long history of the Sheuerman House also shows how conditions and tastes changed over the years. Leopold Sheuerman left it in 1914, and that was well after much of the elite of Des Moines had moved on (to Grand Avenue and south of Grand). The house, like the neighborhood, suffered a slow decline, eventually as a rooming house, later as a halfway house for addicts. It was derelict in 1984 when Dr. Norma Hirsch, who worked at nearby Methodist Hospital, noticed it. Peering through windows, she could see fine woodwork and stenciled ceilings despite peeling paint and water damage. Most of the tower had been torn off.

Dr. Hirsch purchased and started to restore it, first to make it comfortable with modern touches but leaving the ornate walnut woodwork intact. She rebuilt the tower and its pyramid roof, largely to increase the third-floor space but also to restore its original profile. Dr. Hirsch became part of the slow migration that began to turn the neighborhood around. Two decades later, Dr. Hirsch sold the house to York Taenzer, a young preservationist who had already rehabbed and occupied other houses in the neighborhood. Taenzer concentrated on the interior and filled it with a remarkable collection of Victorian furniture, marble fireplaces and other decorative pieces of the period. Amazingly, he investigated past owners and found three pieces of Gothic Revival stained glass that were originally in the Sheuerman House. They're back.

Members of the Sherman Hill Association became close friends and neighbors. Another was Judy McClure, an architect who had rented several houses in the neighborhood and by 1980 bought what she called a five-plex and began its conversion into three apartments. McClure remembers a steep learning curve in terms of construction and many other aspects of preservation. She found out, for example, that banks didn't have much faith in historic neighborhoods, or at least this one at the time. She finally put together a financing arrangement that involved significant federal tax credits. Fortuitously, McClure was offered a position at this time with the State Historic Preservation Office where she would help write new state laws to create additional tax incentives. An important bill along those lines was shepherded by State Representative Jack G. Hatch, another Sherman Hill pioneer.

Even as Sherman Hill took on a new life, rough edges remained and still do. But rough edges have their appeal. David Schlarmann and Shauneen Linton, for example, moved into and restored a large Queen Anne on Center Street in 1998. It took years to strip the clapboard siding and repaint, but the neighborhood suited them; David could walk to work downtown, and Shauneen was close to Hoyt Sherman Place, where she played with the Des Moines Symphony.

A decade later, Schlarmann and Linton noticed a for sale sign on a nearby house on Sixteenth Street. It was a large, brick duplex that was empty, stripped down and neglected. But it was not unknown. It was the Garver House, built in 1895 by a hardware man who got rich in coal mining. The house fell on hard times by the mid-twentieth century and would have been torn down in the 1980s if the Sherman Hill Association had not tested its political muscle and forced the city to save it. It stood derelict for another decade before investors came in with plans, rumor had it, to have some kind of a multifamily commune.

In a stroke of dark luck, the house was seized by federal marshals when someone financing the project was arrested in an embezzlement scheme. Then when the government listed it, Schlarmann looked and got unexpected good news. The previous investors had put in new mechanical systems. With confidence that it was a decent investment, Schlarmann bought it for cash (some $60,000) before he could set up federal and state tax credits and get a bank to finance the rehab. But he had done this before. With patience and by 2014, David and Shauneen had restored (or re-created) its Victorian look and had the house ready to rent on both sides.

Many other Sherman Hill stories are not too different from the Schlarmanns. They are predictable only in the sense that the people who invest sweat equity have an

The Morris Samish House, built in 1892, was a showplace for its first owner, who was a clothing manufacturer. Its Queen Anne lines have been restored to historical accuracy, as have nearly two hundred other houses in the Sherman Hill Historic District. *John Hallstrom photograph. Courtesy of the photographer.*

inordinate passion for the past. As a model of historic preservation, Sherman Hill embodies this and many other many lessons. Rob McCammon, who lives in his second Sherman Hill house (he's moved both from other sites to vacant lots on Sherman Hill) understands the present challenge is less to restore the neighborhood's character than to maintain it. The city's preservation ordinance bans aluminum siding and the like in historic districts. But it requires vigilance.

"In the '70s and '80s, we had people moving to a neighborhood, which wasn't the best, but they loved the architecture," McCammon said. Now Sherman Hill is desirable for other reasons, and many new residents don't understand the importance of restoring to the original design. While Sherman Hill neighbors used to fight drug dealers, now they're up against vinyl windows. Vinyl windows aren't as bad as junkies, McCammon admits. "But in a way we've become a victim of our own success."

Chapter 4

COMMERCIAL DESIGN IN OLD DES MOINES

Des Moines' economic prospects increased after the Civil War, especially in 1866, when the Des Moines Valley Railroad became the first railroad to serve the capital city. Growth was particularly evident on Court Avenue, the main business center by the time the city was large enough to have much business at all. This thoroughfare had the first permanent bridge across the river, which aside from connecting the two sides of town also served curiously as a post for anonymous screeds. A memorable one reminded the city that the East Side near the old Brick Capitol harbored dens of prostitution and crime, perhaps to discourage West Siders from venturing there.

By the 1870s, Court Avenue served a growing list of businesses. At Court and Fourth Street was the B.F. Allen Bank, ensconced in a three-story corner building. Publishing enterprises and hardware stores populated the neighborhood. While a doctor named Aborn invested $14,000 in a lot on Court Street, intending to build an opera house, the doctor subsequently concluded that Des Moines had more transients than demand for high (or even middle) culture, and in 1873 he built a hotel, Aborn House, instead.

The Des Moines Saddlery

Most buildings were rudimentary but not without some niceties of architecture. For example, the Des Moines Saddlery Building, now a carefully restored loft with a microbrewery on the ground floor, features the lines and ornament of the so-called Italianate style. Its first section of four stories went up at Court near Third in 1878, built by the original owner, Jacob Rubelman, who sold saddles and harnesses. Rubelman was practical enough to start with just that one bay (of three windows across), but he did not withhold a heavy cornice at the roofline and elaborate "hood molds" over the windows.

The Des Moines Saddlery was built in many different phases. The benefit of the Italianate style was that it was simple and repetitive enough to make a commercial block built in many phases appear as if built in one. *Steve Foritano photograph.*

The Saddlery's Italianate style was the practical architecture of the American West, of which Des Moines was a part at the time. The style reached vaguely back to the classical tradition, which had a vast repertoire for ornament easily applied to load-bearing brick walls and narrow windows. Italianate details were easily recognized, also easily reproducible. So when the new owner of the Rubelman building, William E. Hoffman, who renamed it Des Moines Saddlery, built two additional bays in 1888, simple repetition of proportion and ornament enabled Hoffman to triple the building's size and make it appear as one.

Italianate buildings could also incorporate touches of modernity, such as it was. The cast-iron façade on the Saddlery's first floor was not just a precursor of the steel frames that would make skyscrapers possible. It created wide openings at street level, making the buildings more inviting from the sidewalk and bringing abundant natural light into storefronts. The cast iron even provided for some decorative swirls to give the business an extra measure of distinction.

This is an old building, and looks it, but as the building grew, it evolved with marks of newer building technology. When the two easternmost bays were constructed in 1888, they had elevators, probably steam-powered. While each of the bays has brick bearing walls, a fifth floor was added in 1901, this one supported by cast-iron columns, providing a clear span of space for the succession of businesses that succeeded after the horse-drawn era. A hat factory, a stove warehouse and a glove company were among concerns that found the Saddlery Building suitable until Court Avenue was abandoned by light industry and, after a hiatus, ready to become a business and entertainment district.

MORE MODERN ROMANESQUE

Nearby on Locust Street stands the Homestead Building, its first part built in 1893, just a little later than the Saddlery but worlds apart in spirit. The Homestead is one of Des Moines' few remaining examples of the Richardsonian Romanesque, marked by strong arches and large windows, as were once seen on many buildings of this vintage in American cities like Des Moines. The Younkers Building and the old Bankers Life Building were larger examples now gone—the latter to fire, the former to make room for a larger modern tower.

Richardsonian buildings were viewed as advanced when they were built, intellectually and even morally. They expressed, said the critics at the time, inherent American characteristics like truth and strength, traits reflected in the use of broad arches, which clearly showed how the walls were held up and also opened the interior to precious natural light. This style was developed most famously by H.H. Richardson

The Homestead Building was built to house the *Iowa Homestead*, an important agricultural publication, in a then-modern Romanesque-style building. *Steve Foritano photograph.*

Opposite: The frank expression of underlying structure, plus large and ample windows, made the Chicago School the precursor of modern architecture as it developed in the twentieth century. *Courtesy of Nelson Construction and Development.*

of Boston, who had turned away from then-fashionable Neoclassical design and joined a movement toward medieval-inspired styles. It was a time when writers and artists lionized the Middle Ages, believing that it exemplified virtues of craftsmanship and individuality, even pure democracy. As American architects sought an American style, many believed that the so-called Romanesque was the answer.

The client of the Homestead Building, James M. Pierce, could not have been blind to these tendencies. He was publisher of the *Iowa Homestead*, one of the most important farm publications of its time. The magazine covered a range of issues from crop rotation to progressive politics; independence, artisanship and, most of all, democracy were values that Pierce and his editor Henry Wallace (grandfather of a future U.S. vice president) actively promoted. It would have made utter sense for the publisher, in meeting with his architect Oliver Smith, to mention that the advanced work of the great Richardson might serve as a model.

Aside from intellectual concerns, the style was well suited to American cities where urban real estate was often expensive and buildings often were built up to, or nearly to, the lot line. The Homestead Building shows the sculptural quality of arches on an

otherwise flat wall. The style also enabled oversized windows—larger than those in the Italianate—to maximize sunlight inside. The short-lived Romanesque—it went out of fashion by 1900—was among the first styles to be associated with "organic architecture," celebrating modest materials like brick, encouraging structural expression and leading to the later Arts and Crafts and Prairie styles.

DANIEL BURNHAM'S FLEMING BUILDING

Less than a decade into the new century, as countless buildings of the Saddlery's and the Homestead's size went up, a significant milestone changed the scale and architectural expectations of downtown Des Moines. It was the Fleming Building, completed in 1907 and the work of the most distinguished architect to build in Des Moines in this period, Daniel Burnham of Chicago. Burnham was a pioneer of the Chicago School, which among other things established the standard that form follows function in large office buildings. Burnham's design is simple, though his history is not; by the time his firm came to Des Moines, its usual style was far more ornamental than the stripped-down commercial buildings that presaged the skyscraper era. In the intervening time, Burnham had been design director of the World's Columbian Exposition in Chicago and became a leader in America's renewed embrace of Neoclassicism. Nevertheless, the Fleming Building, while late in Burnham's career, exhibits a straightforward simplicity that made Chicago the true birthplace of modern architecture.

Guidebook descriptions of the Fleming Building tend to discount the Fleming as stock Burnham fare. In 1902, after all, he had done New York's unmistakable Flatiron Building, and in 1907, he completed Washington's marvelous Union Station, both highly ornamental. Yet the Fleming Building is an excellent example of the Chicago style that became famous worldwide. It is not ornate or uniquely eye catching; rather it is simple and perfectly proportioned. The street level (base) is of human scale with space for stores. The main body (shaft) of the building suggests a place of active business behind large uniform (democratic) glass windows. The top (capital) is a light cornice that dissolves into the sky, defers to the sky, does not compete with it.

As far as Des Moines was concerned, nothing like the Fleming had been done before—it was one of the first steel-frame buildings in the city—and nothing so impressive to the historic eye was done later. The question is why, when Burnham was building much fancier buildings elsewhere, did he (and his firm) design something

Opposite: The Fleming Building's ornament was spare but useful as a way to highlight the second floor's premium well-lighted space. *Courtesy of Nelson Construction and Development.*

so straightforward here? One answer lies in the character of the clients, the Fleming brothers, who do not come off as ornamental types at all. They were life insurance agents, very successful ones, but "hustlers," as the press called them in a complimentary way. They were not merchant princes attempting to glorify themselves, and the result of their fine building serves as proof that the most economic architecture can also be the most elegant.

THE TEACHOUT BUILDING

As the twentieth century progressed, architectural ambition in Des Moines increased, as evidenced also by the Hippee Building (1913) and the Hubbell Building (1913) of the same scale as Fleming, though more decorative. But distinction was not simply a matter of height and certainly not of ornament. For example, investor Horace Teachout became the client for a new building on the East Side of only six stories, but in it he got a masterly proportioned building while also pioneering a new technology for Des Moines: the poured concrete frame. Its style was as simple and unembellished as the Fleming Building. The Teachout's architects, Proudfoot, Bird and Rawson, who were about to embark on the most important period of that firm's illustrious career, gave the innovative structure a simple profile that has stood the test of time.

Horace Teachout, who invested in electric railways and telephones in Des Moines, wanted a practical building. Its concrete frame, while less tested than one of steel, was less expensive and thought to be fireproof, which would have been important for the hotel that was contemplated for the building (but never put in). The first floor had large display windows made possible because the building was held up not by exterior bearing walls but from within. A bank in which Teachout was a partner ultimately went in the second floor, which had appropriately ornate plasterwork.

The Teachout Building, completed in 1912, illustrates the essential modesty of its owner and of the city at this time, not long after a bank disaster of 1907. And as time passed, the Teachout Building continued to be a focal point of the changing East Side. It was one of the tallest buildings in the neighborhood for decades, bringing a certain urbanity to the village-like atmosphere of the neighborhood without spoiling it. Later, the building's fortunes dipped, paralleling those of the East Side at large. In the 1960s,

Opposite: The Teachout Building was a focal point on the East Side, here pictured in the 1930s. *Courtesy of Knowles Blunck Architecture.*

both took a heavy hit when the MacVicar Freeway cut the community in half. Decline accelerated, and many buildings emptied out.

Then in the 1990s, when Des Moines was focusing on the Western Gateway, an eastern entry to the city was being discussed as well. Very little was happening, however. "I got tired of the talk," said Kirk Blunck, then of the leading architecture firm Herbert Lewis Kruse Blunck, so he bought the derelict Teachout Building for $97,000.

Little by little, it became what he imagined. Its size and simplicity made restoration practical if not easy. As for tenants, "it showed the power of the creative class to change things," Blunck said. A high-end furniture store went in and outpaced all expectations. Restaurants have been Teachout tenants, and the *Iowan* magazine put its editorial offices there for a while. Tenants suited the spirit of the building, which had loft-like spaces inside with the look of age on the metalwork and wood. Early in the restoration process, Blunck said, law firms and accounting firms sometimes inquired, eager to get in on what looked like East Side gentrification. Then the owner saw what they wanted to do, which was to break the floors into small offices. Blunck told them that they would be happier elsewhere.

Grass-roots development made real transformation of the Teachout Building's neighborhood come slowly. Even after 2000, there were battles to save, not raze, a number of old buildings. But ten years or so later, this part of the East Side was renamed East Village, and the creative class had made it Des Moines' smartest and most vital neighborhood.

Chapter 5

REMEMBERING PIETY HILL

Pattern books were more prevalent than trained architects in the late 1800s throughout America, and certainly in Des Moines. Most buildings were designed without architects, with clients and builders showing one another pictures in books, sometimes buying actual plans through the mail. The result was often a mix of styles, sometimes finely wrought, other times quickly forgotten when the buildings fell or were torn down.

A few trained architects did get established in early Des Moines, and when they did, they were often favored with commissions to build churches. Devoted parishioners, divinely motivated and financially able, felt that their houses of worship deserved a measure of studied elegance, and quite a few hired William Foster, whose story we touched on as the presumed designer of Hoyt Sherman Place. The Cathedral Church of St. Paul at High and Ninth Streets was one Foster church, the only one still standing in Des Moines. Built in 1883, its solid design reflects Foster's worldly background, which reached back to New York.

Foster, born on Long Island, began his career in the office of Richard Upjohn, architect of Trinity Church on Wall Street in Manhattan (and also author of a popular pattern book for churches). Upjohn was among the first in America to fully embrace the Gothic Revival, then the preferred style for churches in England. The Gothic style became predominant in America, too, as critics expressed the view that it recalled the medieval era, a time of chivalry and moral uplift. But Foster must have been unsure at first if architects were needed in Des Moines at all. When he got off the stagecoach in 1867, the innkeeper where he slept the first night said he might as well go back East. Whatever niceties that architects brought weren't needed.

Time proved the innkeeper wrong, of course, and in little more than a decade, the churches of Piety Hill were going up. Of the eight that were once on the slope north of downtown, Foster and Liebbe (Henry Liebbe being the firm's junior partner) or

Above: This early twentieth-century photo shows Piety Hill, a neighborhood of seven churches and a synagogue, at its height. *Vintage photograph courtesy of John McGinnis.*

Left: St. Paul Episcopal reached heavenward with a spire that no longer exists. *Vintage photograph courtesy of John McGinnis.*

Foster alone designed four of them: Central Christian, Plymouth Congregational, First Methodist and St. Paul's. Each of the four, plus three other churches and a synagogue, had something of the Gothic's skyward reach in their architecture. Only St. Paul remains, and whether or not it was the best, it has many classic features of what is now remembered as "Victorian Gothic." A steep-pitched roof characterized that late nineteenth-century style, especially in the West. Also typical was the multichrome exterior—in this case, reddish granite with limestone accents. Its massing includes a bell tower and gabled porches, all tucked compactly on its corner lot, which was nearly as tight when built as it is now.

Critics have lamented that St. Paul's pointed-arch windows are too wide for their height in terms of the most refined Gothic. This is arguable, though Foster was clearly practical enough to break some European rules to get more light into the church. Complaints are also leveled against the interior—too stout, purists say—though practicality again was important in opening the largest possible sanctuary in limited space. Cast-iron columns also serve the same need, as masonry might have been more "Gothic" in profile but less practical given the availability of metal. Foster was certainly a pragmatist as an architect, and the survival of this church, while so many others on Piety Hill have been torn down, argues heartily against the supposed defects in his design.

There could be many reasons why St. Paul's alone has survived on Piety Hill. (The Methodists are in a newer church on the edges of the district.) One was that it was not condemned by the city as roads were straightened—this being the Presbyterian church's fate. Another is that St. Paul's became increasingly important to the central city as other churches left for more suburban climes. Also convincing is the congregation's love of its collection of stained-glass windows, all donated by parishioners, many of whom were founding members of the church. Some of these names are very well known, such as Hoyt Sherman, who was a vestryman off and on and a singing member of the congregation. "He carried *Te Deum* and *Gloria in Excelcius* through with commendable zeal," wrote another parishioner who knew him.

Sherman contributed the Rose Window at the front of the church and back of the nave. It is St. Paul's most prominent stained-glass work, a circular floral design fit within a pointed-arch window. The work was executed by the distinguished firm of Groves and Steil of Philadelphia in an Arts and Crafts style, generally bolder and more sinuous than the usual hard geometry of the Gothic. One can see its modernity in the way it prefigures Art Nouveau. In 1974, a bomb blast by social dissidents damaged the Rose Window, which was repaired with some changes, but the spirit of its design was restored.

Windows in the west and east walls verge on the modern in other ways, as they combine a figurative quality along with the more traditional geometric designs of a stricter Gothic Revival. A window donated by George M. and Eliza Hippee, son-in-law

The Hippee window, rare in Gothic Revival stained glass for its figurative depiction of nature. *Courtesy of Vicki Ingham.*

and daughter of Jefferson Polk, has rigorous geometric patterns surrounding a scene of birds in flight. (Nature scenes are generally more common in other denominations, such as Congregationalist, say specialists in this field.)

However one interprets it, the glasswork in St. Paul's remains the most constant element of this church. Elsewhere changes have been made in the building, though never so much as to alter the Gothic spirit of the place. When High Street was lowered early in the twentieth century, stone steps to the front door were added. A steeple once surmounted the tower, but when it was damaged by a storm, it was pulled down. There must have been ambivalence about replacing it, as a skeletal steel steeple went up in 1967 but remained for only a decade or so. No ambivalence was expressed when the church purchased a new organ in 1993—a Casavant Opus 3719 and a landmark instrument in the Midwest. The new organ's purchase and placement were at least partially inspired by St. Paul's designation as a cathedral the year before, which meant that the old organ would have to be moved in any case to make room for the *cathedra*, or bishop's chair.

With a stately bearing but modest (save for the glass) detailing, St. Paul's still evokes something of Iowa's most famous Gothic image, *American Gothic*, the 1930 painting by Grant Wood. That painting's reputation has increased over the years, and it is now regarded as a symbol of simplicity and durability, qualities that the architect of St. Paul's certainly had in mind as he designed it.

St. Ambrose Cathedral

Just east of old Piety Hill and still serving the Catholic Diocese of Des Moines is St. Ambrose Cathedral, completed in 1891 (and designated a cathedral in 1911). Medieval architecture was also a common fashion for Catholics at the time, and that preference was affirmed by longtime pastor Father John Brazil when he sent to Chicago for architect James Egan to design it. Egan, born in Ireland, had, like Foster, worked in Richard Upjohn's office in New York and then moved to Chicago after the Great Fire. Having been with Upjohn, Egan possessed indisputable knowledge of Gothic design, preferred in this period for urban churches and which he used for several major churches in Chicago. For variety's sake, he developed a related taste for the Romanesque, which St. Ambrose certainly is.

Gothic and Romanesque architecture lived side by side for much of this period, Gothic reaching more directly to European models, Romanesque being more malleable to originality. There was a third style to choose from at the time, the Neoclassical, especially popular for Catholic churches, which preferred to reach more directly to Rome. In fact, pure styles were hardly de rigeuer; many church

St. Ambrose, designed by Chicago architect James Egan in the Romanesque style. *Courtesy of Catholic Diocese of Des Moines.*

architects combined styles, as Egan himself did in his Sacred Heart Cathedral in Davenport (1891), an unabashed hybrid of Gothic and Romanesque styles. Nevertheless, St. Ambrose's purity—simple exterior and broad vaulted ceiling inside—belies a fussy critic from the 1970s who called it "an undistinguished expression of the Richardsonian Romanesque."

The cathedral's simplicity shows (albeit circuitously) how the Romanesque became an early inspiration for the development of modernism. On the leading edge of architecture at the time, Louis Sullivan and John Wellborn Root both found Romanesque models suitable for architecture as it sought a distinctively American style. The Romanesque was robust with stone walls and solid arches that seemed American in character. Moreover, its parts could be assembled in diverse ways as need and taste demanded. The Romaneseque was "organic," a term suggesting that it was driven by nature and not artificial rules. While St. Ambrose is not about to be mistaken for something modern, it asserts an American character of strength and clarity of form.

The Romanesque was praised for its strength and frank expression of construction. It also harked to Europe and the seat of the Catholic Church. *Courtesy of Catholic Diocese of Des Moines.*

An Unexpected Neighbor

While certainly unintended, St. Ambrose has embraced a neighbor of much more recent architectural distinction that does nothing except enhance the church's own noble design. In 1993, the diocesan offices of the Bishop of Des Moines moved into a former bank building designed by one of modernism's greats, Ludwig Mies van der Rohe. Structural purity, not to mention the ideal of perfect proportion, was the objective in the Home Federal Savings and Loan building across the street from the church. It was completed in 1962, between the time when another Mies building, Meredith Hall, was conceived in 1961 and completed on the Drake campus in 1965. Interlocking boards between university and the savings and loan were likely responsible for selecting the Home Federal building's architect.

The expression is typically Miesian—a steel frame with structural members visible and glass windows filling most of the space between. Curiously, Mies had originally proposed a striking variation on this design for Home Federal—one with two giant trusses above the second-floor banking room, holding the building aloft without interior supports. The bank opted for a more standard Miesian building, ultimately, with a third floor that could be occupied by rent-paying tenants. What is marvelous about this building is the way the first floor, recessed and glassed in, opens generously to the plaza on the two street sides. This feature also provides broader views of the church across the street to the north.

The simplicity of the diocesan Pastoral Center, as the Mies building is now called, reveals the confidence that the architect had in his and his office's mastery of proportion—hence their ability to design so simply and with repose comparable, some say, to the Acropolis in Greece. Less hyperbolically, perhaps, the building exhibits unsurpassed precision in the way steel, glass and brick are assembled. Mies's Des Moines clients were well aware of the kind of architecture that would come with the Home Federal and Drake buildings. What they may not have anticipated was how this business building would enhance the church's profile, and vice versa.

Chapter 6

GRAND AVENUE AND SOUTH OF GRAND

Jefferson Scott Polk, one of Des Moines' early leading citizens, was described as "an inspiring example of justice, charity and consideration." This, admittedly, appeared in his obituary, yet one senses that no one used such terms to describe his partner and rival, B.F. Allen, who lived his life large if not recklessly. Their different personalities help explain the difference between the houses that they built for themselves. Allen's Terrace Hill, as we have seen, was meant to call attention to its owner. Polk's house, Herndon Hall, was more a house designed for the comfort of his family and friends.

As a lawyer, financier and streetcar magnate, Polk would have a luxurious home, but when he built Herndon Hall in 1881, Allen's fall had already occurred and was highlighted by the extravagance of his house. Polk was more careful, and Herndon Hall—not so modest that it did not merit a name—suited Polk's reticence. As restraint often inspires the best architecture, he ultimately got a "superb, almost prototypical [example] of the residential Queen Anne," as described when it was nominated to be placed on the National Register of Historic Places in 1977. It is superb largely because it avoids excess.

Unlike Allen, Polk did not bring a leading architect in from out of town. Rather, he probably found his house's architecture, or a picture of something like it, in a magazine. The architect for Herndon Hall was from New Jersey, Thomas A. Roberts of Newark, whose houses were illustrated in magazines such as *Scientific American*. Roberts was skilled at drafting houses of picturesque charm, with clusters of gables, chimneys and finials that defined Queen Anne houses. He published them and seems to have had a good mail-order business.

When Polk had plans for his house in hand, he delivered them to his local architect, in this case one of the leading firms in town, that of William Foster and Henry Liebbe. Foster and Liebbe were well versed in all fashionable styles, including the Second Empire (as done for the Redhead and probably Sherman houses) and the Gothic

Given its owner's wealth and his times, Jefferson Polk's Herndon Hall represented a restrained architecture and a relatively modest man. *Courtesy of Bergman Folkers Plastic Surgery.*

Herndon Hall's Queen Anne detail was an excellent example of the style in its day. *Courtesy of Bergman Folkers Plastic Surgery.*

Revival (St. Paul's Episcopal). They certainly knew the Queen Anne style, which was popular in the better neighborhoods such as Sherman Hill.

Herndon Hall, like most Queen Annes, has a handmade feel, wrought by brick, stone and fine carpentry. It is somehow more accessible than other styles, especially the Second Empire. From the outside, one witnesses Herndon Hall and can imagine a family entering through the porte-cochere and occupying rooms inside defined by bays and dormers. Even exterior ornament suggests a kind of joy in the house, in its building and living in it. Not that this was a common home or a vernacular design. Bas-relief panels, oriels and brackets were carved by experienced carpenters, yet it was impressive more for the joy it expressed than the expense.

The craftsmanship of the house also calls attention to the many hands involved in building it, and this is especially true on interior finishes, which (as at Terrace Hill) are marked by natural wood and detailed millwork. The parlor has white maple; the music room, red gum. The third-floor ballroom has a colonnade around the perimeter, a feature that one can be sure Polk did not build for his own amusement (he was fifty in 1881) but rather for friends. It may be helpful to view the design of Herndon Hall through the lens of Polk's generosity, a quality also reflected by his funeral, in which employees, not fellow oligarchs, were pallbearers.

A HOUSE BY THE BOOK

In a time and in a city where fashions could change, Victorian architecture provided enough variety to remain current for at least two decades. Until the national depression of 1893, architects continued to set sights on the Queen Anne style with gables, turrets, porches and chimneys in countless variations. Des Moines was not too different from other cities of its size, and its citizens were active readers of books and magazines for the right design from an architect, often from afar.

George F. Barber of Knoxville, Tennessee, was one such architect who published books, actually catalogues, which he used as a marketing technique for his designs. He had dozens to choose from, and when he made a sale he often modified the plans to the taste of customers—customers such as Christopher Huttenlocher, who built his new home on property on Twenty-seventh Street. Huttenlocher was manager of Frederick Hubbell's real estate firm and evidently got the lot from his boss, who had recently subdivided the land around Terrace Hill. Huttenlocher sent away for Barber's design "No. 36" in his book entitled *Cottage Souvenir No. 2*.

Correspondence indicates that Barber charged fifty dollars for a set of plans that could be given to the builder, almost as if the architect were on site. Barber may not have known the lay of the land where his houses were built, but he definitely got to know something of his clients. "We have carried the staircase out a little ways, as per your request," Barber wrote Huttenlocher as modified drawings were being prepared for Des Moines. He also created a customized rounded tower at one corner of the house with an uncommon two-story veranda. What has not changed in No. 36 is the

The Huttenlocher House, on the edge of the Owl's Head neighborhood, was a customized design for a client who probably never met his architect. *Courtesy of Knowles Blunck Architecture.*

profile. The roofline is complex and picturesque; it keeps Barber's promise that his homes were "artistic."

Once again, it was a credit to the architect and to the client, also to good fortune, that this house survived the passing fashion for the Victorian. As we know from Sherman Hill, the twentieth century began with a tendency toward simplicity, and this was hardly a simple house. That it remains is attributable to a number of factors. One was that its verticality made it suited to its compact site on the edge of Owl's Head (now a historic district). Also in favor of the house was that it continued to suit Huttenlocher's daughter-in-law who lived here until the 1980s. Fae Huttenlocher was a gardening editor for *House and Garden*. Then there was the good fortune of the subsequent owners, Jeff and Janet Hunter, who came to the house with a sense of history and architecture. Jeff was owner of the historic Hotel Fort Des Moines, and the couple even sent to New York for a designer who could enlarge the house in a renovation that encloses a part of the wraparound porch without bastardizing the design.

THE CRAWFORD AND COFFEE HOUSES

Imagining Grand Avenue around 1900 before it was commercialized provides an evolving picture of architectural fashion. An example of change was a neighbor of the Huttenlocher and Polk Houses, the Crawford House, just a couple blocks east of Herndon Hall. R.A. Crawford's home, designed by Liebbe, Nourse and Rasmussen (successor to William Foster's firm) and completed in 1896, shows that the trend toward simpler lines was only partly economic. It was also driven by a continued effort to create an architecture that could be called "American." A popular approach at this time was that of H.H. Richardson of Boston, who built houses of rusticated stone walls and fortress-like stability. The Crawford House, which also has good dose of Neoclassical detail, was hardly a pure example of the so-called Richardsonian Romanesque. But its medieval massing was definitely influenced by it.

Another sign of the up-to-date-ness of the Crawford House was its spacious and flowing interior, with broad arches delineating and not dividing rooms. This was different from the smaller closed-off interior spaces that often filled Victorian houses not too many years out of fashion. Plus, Crawford's home had a prominent first-

The Coffee Mansion, home of patent-medicine tycoon Dr. Coffee, in the Chateauesque style, was more durable than the owner's ability to stay there. *Vintage photo courtesy of John McGinnis.*

floor library, a definite sign of the times. One objective of modern design in this period was to highlight unique qualities of the client in architecture. Libraries became centerpieces in some such houses, different from older Queen Annes, where they were hidden away or disguised as parlors. Significantly, the Crawford House was featured in a 1907 *Midwestern* magazine article on libraries in Des Moines homes. While the literary tastes of Mr. Crawford, a banker, were not specified, his library had an Arts and Crafts feel (with touches of folk art), which marked him as a man of distinctly up-to-date tastes.

A similar house from the same time, farther west on Grand, was the mansion of Dr. W.O. Coffee. Whether or not the doctor, a physician and entrepreneur, had modernity in mind, he was definitely interested in a striking trophy that would reflect his considerable wealth. His line was patent medicines, and among his better-known products was a solution for cataracts. Business was very good for a while, and success was exuded by his home, which, like the Crawford House, approached the Richardsonian Romanesque in style.

In fact, this house is more "Chateauesque," a variation that reached back to Gilded Age mansions in New York and from there to the castles of the Loire Valley in France. While American homes were very typically a blend of many styles, the Coffee Mansion's unmistakable note is the immovable strength that architects rendered for self-made men and their families. In fact, the house was more immovable than Dr. Coffee, who ran into legal troubles related to the efficacy of his products and left town. After the style had passed, the house remained and remains an artifact out of time, impressive but somehow as antiquated as the patent medicine business that built it.

English Fantasy in Stone

Styles continued to change as the Queen Anne, the Romanesque and the Chateauesque came and went. By the Roaring Twenties, other design ideas were having their day. Georgians were popular as America was reasserting its identity. Variants of the Prairie School influenced some houses. But for the well-heeled in the new century's first prosperity boom, there was the English Tudor, the deeply historical style modernized and made famous in England toward the end of the nineteenth century by the hand of architect Norman Shaw.

In America, English Tudor was also popular and well known from widely published designs by architects such as McKim, Mead and White of New York and Ralph Adams Cram of Boston. The Tudor style's long floor plates and front-facing gables were practical because they were asymmetrical. Just as importantly, it suited America's desire to reach back to English roots, this in the face of mass migration from Eastern

One aspect of the Tudor style's appeal in the past was that additions could be made to a house at will without upsetting the architecture's asymmetrical balance. Salisbury House affected this sense of age for its client, Carl Weeks. *Laura Sadowsky photograph. Courtesy of Salisbury House.*

and Southern Europe. The result was that half-timbered houses built in the first half of the twentieth century are prolific in nearly every city in America.

A certain Anglophilia certainly moved Carl Weeks, whose fabulous wealth came as owner of the Armand Company, a maker of women's cosmetics. Weeks began as a country boy from Linn County, Iowa, who moved to Des Moines to study pharmacy. He got involved in patent medicines and cosmetics and ultimately developed a face powder infused in cold cream that achieved "a degree of uniform coverage and adhesion to the skin," as it was clinically described. Armand's Complexion Powder was a great success, especially after Weeks launched marketing schemes. Armand was an early master of direct mail. It used radio advertising, introduced in the 1920s, and the company is credited with helping reverse female inhibitions about beautifying cosmetics with slogans such as "The Creed of Beauty."

Having made a fortune by the early 1920s, Weeks and his wife, Edith, embarked on living the life that it afforded them. As for a house, they initially considered something in a Mediterranean style to build on his rolling site south of Grand. He went so far as to have the local firm of Boyd and Moore prepare sketches in that manner. Then in 1922 the Weekses visited England and were enchanted by a particular country estate called King's House in Salisbury, Wiltshire. It was a classic Tudor mansion built over a period of several hundred years. Back in Des Moines, Weeks explained to his architects that what appealed to him now was that house's Tudor window, glazing nearly an entire two-story bay. He was also enchanted by the Norman porch, a veranda with a room (or part of one) in the projecting gable overhead.

Weeks's preference for the picturesque must have pleased architect Byron Bennett Boyd, who was also an artist. As a young man, Boyd had studied painting at Provincetown, Massachusetts, and then chose architecture as a profession, getting a degree at Columbia University and eventually landing in Des Moines with Proudfoot, Bird and Rawson in 1914. Two years later, he went off on his own with partner Herbert Moore, and they were successful for a decade. In fact, Boyd regarded painting as his true calling, and he did reasonably well at that. A *Tribune-Capital* article in 1929 explained that he had a romantic inclination and "preferred to paint castles more than skyscrapers."

Boyd's affection for Tudor was evident in his own house, nearby at the corner of Forty-second and Greenwood, near Salisbury House, as the Weeks home would be called. Boyd's design for himself was intricately half-timbered, and the array of exposed timbers was adzed to give a rough-hewn effect and sandblasted to simulate age. About his interest in historic models of architecture, he explained to another reporter, "What is modern today is gone tomorrow, but no man has done justice to the masters."

History was also what Weeks wanted. "If this house doesn't look one hundred years old the day it is finished, we have failed," he told his stone carver. That craftsman remembered that when they visited the limestone quarry in Indiana, they tried to choose the most weathered and marked blocks they could find. Brick used in Salisbury House, moreover, was salvaged from demolitions on High Street (perhaps from Piety Hill churches), and Weeks instructed that "there must be some irregularity in the laying to produce the best effect."

The house may not have even been started in 1923 when the owner brought on another architect, William Whitney Rasmussen, of New York (brother of Edward F. Rasmussen, of the firm that designed the Crawford House). Perhaps previous progress was slow, though Boyd was not fired. At any rate, Rasmussen came in and convinced Weeks that his ambitions for his house outstripped his $150,000 budget. Rasmussen also suggested that additional funds could be found in the Armand Company, and the house could be impressively used in advertising. Salisbury House would become "an Armand institution."

With that, a financial floodgate opened, and the architects made trips to the south of England to absorb the ambiance of the place Weeks loved. They also met English antiques dealer Reginald Mullins, a Rotarian like Weeks, who suggested that architectural elements could be salvaged from old buildings then being torn down in Salisbury. Floorboards and beams in Salisbury House's large Commons Room are "period" elements and give this interior, impressive for its size and Old Master paintings, the look of unmistakable age.

Also from Salisbury, from the town's White Hart Inn, came the marvelous sixteenth-century rafters in Weeks's Great Hall, the main entry, with its Gothic-like vertical reach and a high balcony at the back. At some point during these salvage jobs for Weeks in Salisbury, workmen found a plaque with the inscription, "C. Weekes 1580." This excited Carl Weeks considerably; he inlaid the plaque in the

The south door of Salisbury House was fashioned of knapped flint, a rough and ancient technique inspired in this case from King's House in England. *Laura Sadowsky photograph. Courtesy of Salisbury House.*

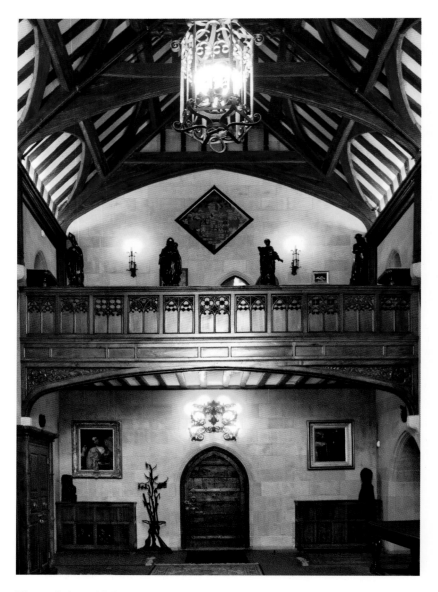

The south door of Salisbury House was fashioned of knapped flint, a rough and ancient technique inspired, in this case, by King's House in England. *Laura Sadowsky photograph. Courtesy of Salisbury House.*

Great Hall and spent time and treasure attempting, unsuccessfully, to establish a connection to his hoped-for forebearer.

Salisbury House is an archetypal Tudor Revival house, simulating age with the inherently organic Tudor form—the quality of asymmetricality and seeming randomness

Weeks was a devoted book collector, thus his library was perhaps the most personal room in this house. The paneling and other fittings are from the sixteenth-century English house of one C. Weekes, no apparent relation. *Laura Sadowsky photograph. Courtesy of Salisbury House.*

that makes it appear to have been added on to over the decades and even centuries. Its most ageless element, a section of knapped flint masonry, replicates something of the same in King's House: a wall of rough flint stones set in mortar. Around the main door to the garden the knapped flint is used in the same wall with irregular limestone blocks. At ninety years, it looks centuries old, as it likely did when built.

The house, also its art collection and books, gave the Weeks family great pleasure, so that when when the Armand Company faced serious reversals, the owner occupied himself with how to keep his home intact. In 1934, it became the property of Drake University, which used it for its art department while members of the Weeks family also lived here. Then in 1954, the Iowa State Education Association purchased the house for its headquarters. That continued until 1999, when a foundation was created to purchase and maintain the house as a museum. Today, Salisbury House allows Weeks's elaborate fantasy to be touched and partially understood by casual visitors.

Streamlined Modern in Des Moines

The disruptions that Carl Weeks suffered in the 1930s were old news in Europe, where World War I had erased a Lost Generation and forced a reassessment of values, including those governing architecture. One response was the design ideas of the Bauhaus, which sought an architecture of pure function, for "the machine age," as the founders of the Bauhaus school put it. Among Bauhaus directors was Ludwig Mies van der Rohe, who would later design two buildings in Des Moines. While still a young man in Germany, Mies wrote that past ideas of design were obsolete and that architecture of the twentieth century must be expressed in unadorned construction. "We reject all aesthetic speculation, all doctrine, all formalism," Mies wrote. "We refuse to recognize problems of form, only problems of building."

While Bauhaus buildings in Germany could be severe unto cold, modernism in America was similar, but it also acquired softer qualities. Beauty and even romance in machine-age buildings were found in streamlining, which actually commenced on a smaller scale in buildings, rather than in industrial design, and migrated into architecture. Streamlining's pioneer, Norman Bel Geddes, began as a theatrical designer, and after some period of speculation of what was truly modern, published a book in 1932 entitled *Horizons*. In it he popularized aerodynamic form in trains, cars, appliances and buildings. Bel Geddes's book provided clear inspiration for one of Des Moines' most remarkable houses, the Butler Mansion.

The house for Earl Butler was designed for the wealthy world traveler who said he wanted a house that would inspire him to stay home. Modeled partly after Bel Geddes's drawings but also resembling an ocean liner, the Butler Mansion features the drama of a stage set, with white cast concrete walls, curved interiors, indirect lighting and arrangement of rooms that (unlike convention at the time) put the most important living areas in the back, where they overlooked the countryside.

Kraetsch and Kraetsch, the firm that designed the Butler house, had done nothing like this before in 1936 when the place was completed. But they had a hefty portfolio. Two (of three) Kraetsch brothers studied architecture in the East and put in time with Proudfoot and Bird before going off on their own. Among credits were the Art Deco unto rococo theater at Hoyt Sherman Place (completed in 1923 with their partner at the time Norman Vorse) and the Capitol (later Paramount) Theater building on Grand Avenue.

Theatrical itself, the Butler interior is bisected by a ramp that switches back and forth through the space of four floors. This feature recalls Corbusier, if not for function then for visual effect. If nothing more, the house proves that America would exit the Great Depression with a new approach to architecture. It also demonstrated that Kraestch and Kraetsch had what the best Des Moines architects always had, which was versatility as well as skill.

Des Moines architecture was rarely so elaborate as the Butler Mansion, and it was hardly ever so advanced. But it is obvious that something was happening there that would guide design for the rest of the century. Modernism in its many forms was concerned with "volume not mass," as sometimes explained. It concentrated on the spaces inside with thin and often glassy walls to enclose it. The seductive advantage,

The Butler Mansion became one of the nation's best-known streamlined residences, designed for a world traveler who wanted a house that would make him content to stay home. *Courtesy of Library of Congress Prints and Photographs Division.*

The Butler Mansion dramatically introduced Des Moines to a modernist future in the '30s. *Courtesy of the Integer Group.*

The Trier House, a Usonian house by Frank Lloyd Wright, with unique sensations of space and light that are typical of the architect. *Courtesy of the Douglas M. Steiner collection, Edmonds, WA.*

of course, was savings, and as America moved to the suburbs, modernism went hand in hand with track housing, prefab and other housing approaches of the postwar economic boom.

There were costs, however. A non-monetary one that we see vividly in Des Moines is the loss of something indispensable just a few decades before. That was the front porch, large in Victorian-era houses, shrunk in Tudor Revival architecture and all but disappeared in modernism. With front porches went an element of community building. Social insulation became an unintended consequence of modernity, and it took architects decades to even notice before before any of them even attempted to rectify it.

ICONS OF MID-CENTURY MODERN

It was not just tract houses with plate-glass picture windows that reflected the preference for isolation. Iconic mid-century houses show the same tendency. The Trier House, one of many Frank Lloyd Wright buildings in Iowa but the only one within Des Moines' orbit, did have a striking relationship to the outdoors. But for Wright, the outdoors meant nature and not neighbors.

When Dr. Paul Trier, a Des Moines physician, contacted Wright to design this house, the architect advised that the Triers find a site as far out of the city as possible. It was probably Wright's anti-urban bias talking, but his warning that the Triers would be followed by other home-builders turned out to be true. In fact, Wright never saw the site, only photos that the clients sent. What he gave them was a house, completed in 1958, that is inconspicuous from the street to the north and opens luxuriously to the downward slope to the south.

Wright used his "Usonian" template here, which was a simple layout and palette of materials that enabled homeowners to have Prairie Style houses on a reasonable budget. This one, like most other Usonians, uses the brick and wood that Wright and his clients loved, plus the complex geometry that could give even small interior spaces plenty of light and the feeling of space. Some of that geometry is applied to the exterior as well—though alterations made by Wright associates after his death conceal these. All told, we see here that Wright was a consummate modernist who created a cozy familial environment, which he obviously valued, but no apparent affection for neighbors.

The antipathy toward neighbors was not entirely an architectural preference. It was a real estate phenomenon as well, as suburban development sought larger lots and, in the Southern Hills neighborhood not too far from Fleur Drive, broad views. That was certainly what lawyer and entrepreneur Harold Goldman was buying when he moved to Southern Hills Drive to a house that was designed by Richard Neutra, an Austrian who had moved to California after a brief stint working for Frank Lloyd Wright.

Neutra's residences were hardly insular, as his "California Modern style" was designed for enjoyment of the outdoors. We see this in the Goldman House, completed in 1962, where porch and gardens seem almost to penetrate the interior and show that even in the harsh Iowa climate the clients valued the out-of-doors. While views of neighbors are limited, a good panorama of downtown Des Moines was arranged from the house. And a large site otherwise bereft of geological character had a large boulder introduced to the front yard, courtesy of the architect.

In some ways, the Neutra's Goldman House is something of an intellectual exercise, but one that has stood the test of time and enjoyment, as one of the Goldmans' sons still lives there.

Chapter 7

DES MOINES' CITY BEAUTIFUL MOVEMENT

The Des Moines River represents a feature of incalculable importance to the city, but not always in a predictable way. The origins of Des Moines can be traced to the creation of Fort Des Moines, built in 1843 where the big river met the Raccoon. The fort housed soldiers charged with monitoring the Sauks and Meskwakis, Native American tribes moved to the area from eastern Iowa. In limited ways, the river connected the settlement with the rest of the world. Canoes were suitable most of the time, and steamboats could channel through for some five months of the year.

Before too many decades passed, the river assumed an even more significant role, if not entirely positive, as the dividing line between the two sides of the city. From an early point in their history, the East and West Sides either opposed or ignored each other, with the result that the river became a no-man's land, neglected and undesirable. That was until the more genteel elements of the city voiced a desire to improve the cultural and visual tenor of Des Moines, and for them, at the dawn of the twentieth century, improving the riverfront became symbolic. As plans took form, the river—both sides—represented the intended centerpiece of a new Civic Center of government.

Des Moines was growing wealthy as a center of manufacturing and finance. With wealth came leisure, and with leisure came progressive ideas such as the planning principles of the City Beautiful movement. City Beautiful was an idea that encouraged fast-growing American cities to avoid laissez faire chaos with fine public buildings and broad boulevards in strategic places. Leaders of the movement realized such plans would facilitate flow through the city, inspire civic pride and encourage private property owners to design their buildings with equal care. In Des Moines, City Beautiful inspired the Public Library, the Municipal Building, the old post office and other stately structures. It inspired graceful bridges across the river and, in time, more stately avenues that crossed those bridges.

The Des Moines Public Library of 1903, now restored as home of the World Food Prize. *Courtesy of World Food Prize.*

DES MOINES WOMEN'S CLUB VISITS THE FAIR

An early episode of the City Beautiful movement came in 1893 when the Des Moines Women's Club traveled to the World's Columbian Exposition to visit the "White City," an early great example of American city planning. Its magnificence—with immense palaces designed by the nation's leading architects—was obvious to anyone who witnessed it. Its example motivated the leaders of many growing cities to bring order and beauty to their own, which if left to economic utility or chance would have neither.

On the train to Chicago, one imagines, the Women's Club passed the industrial districts of Des Moines' East Side without comment. Coming home was another matter, however, as the women had been dazzled by the power of the fair's Cours d' Honneur with pristine buildings and water features. As they discussed the beauty they had seen in Chicago, they were shocked if not surprised at what they saw out the windows. No sooner had the train passed within view of the State Capitol than Des Moines gave the impression hardly of a White City, but of a *red* city mostly brick, or even a *black* city, covered in soot from the smoke of bituminous coal. Then came the river. If there was anything that distinguished it beyond ramshackle huts it was advertising signs that rose over sagging roofs on both banks. By the time the train

Arched bridges were among the first improvements to the river as Des Moines resolved to develop a Civic Center of government buildings. *Courtesy of Library of Congress Prints and Photographs Division.*

pulled into the depot several blocks west of the river, the women were saying that something ought to be done about bringing public beauty to Des Moines, which was otherwise an economically healthy city.

It would take time to bring a sense of order and beauty to the Des Moines riverfront. But members of the Women's Club, mostly the first generation of "society women" in Des Moines, possessed not just time but also ambition, and they worked, initially behind the scenes, to promote good planning and specifically a more dignified riverfront. It took time, but they got involved in 1900 when the Park Board brought landscape designer Warren H. Manning, formerly of Olmsted & Vaux (designer of New York's Central Park and much of the Chicago fair). Manning had a look and was impressed by the city's prospects. He delivered a report and called Des Moines "exceedingly fortunate in possessing so much of its river frontage in the very heart of the business district." In the City Beautiful manner, he suggested, it should be reserved for public buildings.

The first building of the imagined riverfront, the Public Library, was ready in 1903. It took another six years for the second, the new Post Office. That one was nearly finished when the Women's Club, perhaps impatient, brought another City Beautiful advocate to Des Moines. Charles Mumford Robinson, a journalist who wrote about cities in magazines such as the *Atlantic*, visited, and his report affirmed what Manning had said. He went steps further to detail a plan of broad boulevards radiating out from the river. Riverfront development would be marked by additional government buildings. He wrote, "A row of public buildings on either side, and park—encompassed, will create—almost is creating—a Civic Center of extraordinary excellence."

THE PUBLIC LIBRARY

The riverfront Civic Center (not to be confused with the Des Moines Civic Center auditorium built in the 1970s) developed slowly but with architectural care from the time the cornerstone for the Des Moines Library was laid in 1901. Even before that, it was a sign of political will that the city engineered a three-way transaction to vacate the library site. The library would go on the west bank at Locust, long occupied by the Des Moines arsenal, which in exchange was granted rights to the east bank site that had been set aside for a state museum. With some presumed financial settlement, the museum would later purchase its own land when the state was ready to build. It went smoothly, or somewhat so. A few businessmen objected that the riverfront library would be too far from downtown. Strangely,

The library on the river set the architectural tone for the City Beautiful movement as it unfolded in Des Moines. *Courtesy of Special Collections, Cowles Library, Drake University.*

the Women's Club expressed doubts, perhaps because the Des Moines River was still unbeautiful.

But the library board surged forth, hiring the local architecture firm of Smith and Gutterson for the building's design. It seemed like a natural and safe choice, as senior partner Oliver O. Smith, in his thirties, had distinguished himself as a man of indomitable "energy, united to the highest gifts for his work," as an admirer wrote. Smith was largely self-educated, having acquired architectural credentials through work in construction. The design partner, Frank Gutterson, was a Minnesota boy in his early twenties. He had studied at MIT and the Ecole des Beaux-Arts in Paris and then had a stint in the office of Frank Flagg, an early architect of West Point.

Gutterson also had some library experience. When fresh out of school and in private practice by himself, he had designed the Owatonna, Minnesota library after researching what worked and what did not for libraries of moderate size. He corresponded with librarians and visited many of their buildings, and he learned that the Richardsonian Romanesque, praised by critics at the time as the most advanced American style, was not ideal as far as the people responsible for the books were concerned. Too limited open space, said some, and too low and dark, said others. Gutterson found that Neoclassical design as taught by the Beaux-Arts, which modern architects viewed as old-fashioned, did best what librarians really wanted, which was maximize interior space and natural light.

Smith and Gutterson's Beaux-Arts design, a functional library, retains its utility as a celebratory hall. *Jim Heemstra photograph. Courtesy of World Food Prize.*

Beaux-Arts architects often shaped their work after older existing buildings. In this case, the Des Moines Library was modeled after a small museum in Nancy, France, though this was only a starting point for the design. "No attempt has been made to make a copy of any existing building," wrote the *Des Moines Leader* after seeing plans for the building. The design provided for porticos to the east and west with the main entrance facing the river and a carriage entry facing downtown. Inside, the foyer rotunda was high and wide, the better to fill it with patrons and light, and also so librarians could more easily observe patrons.

If there was anything unique about the library, it was the choice of Kettle River sandstone for the exterior. The more natural choice might have been lighter-colored Bedford limestone from Indiana, widely used for monumental architecture at the time. No specific reason for the stone is documented, but one factor might have been that scores of other libraries, many financed by steel baron Andrew Carnegie, were using Bedford stone at this time. One can speculate that the progressive lights of Des Moines wanted no hint that the city was beholden to Carnegie, whose reputation as a robber baron was very much alive.

"Chaste" was how Gutterson often described his designs, in that they were stately without excessive ornament. This was certainly driven by economics but also by a certain modernity that valued rich materials but plain surfaces. Happily, this simplicity enabled a later addition of WPA murals to the library's blank walls during the Depression. Entitled *A Social History of Des Moines*, the images chronicle Iowa from prehistoric times through to twentieth-century worker struggles. They were revealed and restored when the old library was renovated as headquarters for the World Food Prize Foundation in 2011.

A Splendid Courthouse on the Wrong Site

As the library graced its side of the river, it was natural to encourage the Polk County commissioners to build its new courthouse on the other. As early as 1901, the East Side Merchant's Association tried to lure the county with a site opposite the library. Such an idea seemed reasonable based on long-term planning. But, wrote Johnson Brigham in his 1911 history of Des Moines, "the logic was lost on the [county] board." The new county courthouse went up in 1906 several blocks off the river where an old smaller one had been.

No one seriously accused the county board of graft on this count, and it may simply be chalked up to rivalry between the two sides of town. In any case, when the building was finished, whatever politics colored the affair were largely forgotten because the new courthouse, designed by the local firm of Proudfoot and Bird,

Polk County Courthouse, which undertook to rival the State Capitol in splendor if not size. *Courtesy of Library of Congress Prints and Photographs Division.*

turned out to be a splendid piece of work. The firm, with William Proudfoot handling the business side and George Washington Bird heading the design, set out to build a predictable but striking building. It would have the usual features: Indiana limestone, rigorous symmetry and a clock tower that dominated its part of the city. Also conventional was its scale and monumentality, inspired by the long shadow of the Columbian Exposition. Still, it was meant to be impressive, and it was.

The courthouse reflected both the commissioners' wish to assert their importance among other governmental entities in town and the architects' mastery of Neoclassical form. Among other features, the exuberant clock tower served both. "Courthouse towers visibly attested to the importance of these buildings as temples of justice," wrote architectural historian Wesley Shank in a 1992 article on Iowa courthouses. For Polk County, Proudfoot and Bird unabashedly chose the Giralda Tower atop the Cathedral of Seville, Spain, as its model. It had been used in other Beaux-Arts buildings in this period, including Madison Square Garden in New York and the Wrigley Building in Chicago.

Above, left: Green men, part human with plant-like features, were a convention in architectural ornament reaching to Gothic times and appropriate for Iowa's agricultural setting. *Robert Blink photograph.*

Above, right: Anonymous craftsmen carved faces normally seen only from a distance. *Steve Foritano photograph.*

Right: Dozens of carvings around it give a conventionally beautiful building its mystery. *Robert Blink photograph.*

It was not just the architects who deserve credit for the building. Its stone work, even then a vanishing art, involved the hand of anonymous carvers whose most remarkable work is the twenty-eight grotesques in the keystones of the arches around second- and third-floor windows. In medieval Europe carvers often caricatured their bosses in grotesques and gargoyles, sometimes positioned on

The tower expressed the majesty of government and attempted to keep people on time. *Steve Foritano photograph.*

Above: Lunettes in the courthouse depict great moments in Iowa and American history. *Robert Blink photograph*.

Right: Fittings and details of the courthouse suggest that no cost was spared. *Steve Foritano photograph*.

Metal workers were kept busy in this last robust gasp of the Gilded Age. *Courtesy of Special Collections, Cowles Library, Drake University.*

buildings so as to be invisible to almost anyone. Here the faces are at least faintly visible from the street. But they are not real people, rather mostly "green men," medieval-inspired faces part-human, part-vegetable with leaves and vines growing from faces either comic or threatening.

THE DES MOINES PLAN AND A NEW CITY HALL

Whatever dismay the city fathers felt when the county built away from the river, they remained committed to the City Beautiful vision. Shortly after the courthouse came the post office, south of the library. This must have been an encouragement for those in Des Moines who had been envisioning the Civic Center. The post office, designed by chief federal architect James Knox Taylor, a graduate of MIT who may not have seen Des Moines, brought a thorough Beaux-Arts approach to the design. But it was also up to date.

Today, the Neoclassical post office appears very much like civic buildings in American cities everywhere. But the adaptation of classicism to urban settings was evolving when

The U.S. Post Office, the second Civic Center building on the river, suggested a more utilitarian approach to government. *Courtesy of Special Collections, Cowles Library, Drake University.*

City Hall, or the Municipal Building, was a sober design for a reform-minded government in 1910. *Courtesy of Special Collections, Cowles Library, Drake University.*

this one was built in 1909. Towers were out. "The authoritative connotations of the tower were no longer appropriate for the Progressive Era," which was nigh, wrote Shank. Exterior walls were pushed almost to the street line, and ornament remains spare. It suggested to people who saw it that what was important here was less the striving majesty of the government but the efficient activity conducted within.

The most modern and functional building of the Civic Center is the east bank's Municipal Building. Like the post office, the exterior is classical, dignified but restrained. What is more interesting is the interior, designed as an architectural manifestation of honesty and integrity. Des Moines' city hall, as it is also called, came at a high point for the Progressive Era when the city distinguished itself nationally as a paragon of good government.

The good-government story began around 1907 when a popular vote adopted the commission-form of city government, a radical development at the time. Instead of a bevy of aldermen elected by wards and surrounded by ward-heelers, the commission-form would reduce elective offices to four councilors elected at large. Each of the four would then be made head of a management commission: public services, public safety, finance and administration. The theory was that centralized governance would attract better elected officials and that they would behave in more transparent ways.

Transparency was needed at the time. Like so many cities its size, Des Moines had long eluded reform, and the old city hall was a dark building often described as a "rabbit's warren of graft." One could only imagine the smoke-filled rooms within, it was said. Among its regular visitors were the madams who operated the city's bordellos and who made monthly calls to pay "fines" accrued the previous month. Graft was practiced and concealed with little effort.

The Des Moines Plan, as its commission-form was called, followed what had been called the Galveston Plan, instituted in Texas after that city's catastrophic hurricane. As efforts to rebuild there were impeded by corrupt officials, Galveston centralized government as an emergency measure. In Des Moines, the first city outside of Texas to adopt commission-form, the change embodied the high-mindedness of the same people who were pushing City Beautiful ideas.

Politics rarely unfold neatly, of course, and this story did not. Opposition to the change came from working folk (and their representatives) who regarded the smaller council and more centralized rule as anti-democratic. Then, after the Des Moines Plan was accepted by referendum, most of the slate that the elites put up to fill its centralized offices was defeated. John MacVicar, a former mayor who was not considered one of the elite, was elected, however, and predictably or not, one of his early decisions was to build a new city hall in the city's spirit of reform.

Again, there was no straight line. A bond issue was passed, supposedly to pay for construction. When they were ready to break ground, however, an East Side citizen named Mary Coggeshall intervened. She complained that she was not permitted to vote in the referendum solely because she was a woman, and she sued on the grounds that Iowa law stated that anyone who owned property and paid taxes was entitled to vote, regardless of gender. She was right, a court ruled, and a new vote was taken. The result was the same as before. Des Moines reform was coming slowly but surely.

Next, architectural monkey business had to be squeezed from the project after it came to light that one of the five firms in the running to design the Municipal Building had offered a $2,500 "jackpot" to anyone who could deliver the contract. It took little time for the four commissioners to meet and determine that a consortium of architects would produce the design. It would consist of four firms chosen from the five under consideration—minus the jackpot guys.

Proudfoot and Bird, which had drawn a version of the Municipal Building prior to the Coggeshall challenge, was one of the virtuous four, and the building constructed looked very much like its original design. It was simple and businesslike, like the post office and like other public buildings that would later fill the Civic Center. The building is long and low with simple pilasters around the perimeter. Its profile expressed modest efficiency.

But if the exterior seemed unremarkable at the time, the interior of the Municipal Building was not. The main business floor was wide open, divided only by cages into four quadrants, each for one of the four commissions of government. The "counting room," as it was called, has a gently bowed ceiling overhead and large clerestories, assuring that city business would be done in the full light of day. "No screens, high counters or roll-top desks are found to furnish concealment for idle clerks or political callers," wrote MacVicar, justifiably proud of the building, in the *American City* magazine.

Still admirable, the interior finds beauty in simplicity and the spirit of reform politics. Such overt transparency would not last forever, however, and the Des Moines Plan was converted back to a more conventional form by the 1950s. But that open counting room, now occupied by many city departments, memorializes a moment of political high ambition in Des Moines. It also demonstrates that architecture can still remind us that a golden age of politics, while hardly perfect and never permanent, remains an enduring ambition.

Chapter 8

TALL BUILDINGS OF
THE JAZZ AGE

Des Moines is a rich museum of architecture, especially downtown, where large buildings, confidently wrought, represent a wide spectrum of architecture from the 1920s and '30s. It was a time when urban architecture was varied, on account of technology and a swift succession of styles, culminating in what we know as Art Deco.

Excellent examples of the period's architectural fashions were produced largely, not entirely, by the firm that began as Proudfoot and Bird and that had a number of different names as the decades passed. To understand the skyscraper era in Des Moines is to understand Proudfoot and partners, who were undisputably "the foremost architecture firm in the state," as described by Des Moines architectural historian Barbara Beving Long.

Proudfoot and Bird, with its masterpiece of the Polk County Courthouse, later became Proudfoot, Bird and Rawson. Further name changes—it has survived to the present and goes by Brooks, Borg and Skiles—suggest longevity, but that is only one characteristic of the firm that designed the Hubbell Building, the Hotel Fort Des Moines, the Equitable Building and the Des Moines Building, each in a different style. The firm was successful partly because it boasted connections that made it the frontrunner for any important commission in the early decades of the century. More importantly, architects at the firm understood keenly their times and the influences that were changing commercial architecture.

William Proudfoot, the leading force in the firm in its most important years, was born in Indianola in 1860. He was only a year or two out of high school when he came to Des Moines for a position with Foster and Liebbe, staying there until 1882. That was probably his last position working for anyone else, and since he was eager to capitalize on the mercurial growth of the American frontier, he teamed with another Foster draftsman, George W. Bird, and set out to "barnstorm" the upper Midwest in search of good-sized commissions.

The tower of the Equitable Building as seen from the Des Moines Building deck. *Courtesy of Nelson Construction and Development.*

The partnership's first real strike was the Hughes County Courthouse in Pierre, South Dakota. Completed in 1885 (and now demolished), it was fully a creation of its architectural time: an Italianate structure with weight born by masonry walls, narrow windows and a fancifully concocted tower overhead. After Pierre, Proudfoot took a year in Boston as a special student at MIT. This may have been to improve his drafting skills and to expose himself to a greater variety of influences than would have come naturally at home. The Richardsonian Romanesque, for example, was more or less born in Boston, and MIT, the nation's first true architecture school, was dedicated to the Beaux-Arts style and method of teaching. So Proudfoot, never a great designer, became conversant in these and other major approaches, which he would bring back and use in the West.

While Proudfoot handled the business side of the firm, his partner's interest was in the aesthetic realm. Bird was born in New Jersey in 1854, and while knowledge of his background is sketchy, it appears he moved to Philadelphia, where he worked in a woodworking mill, "hence his ability to design detailed interior," according to Barbara Long, who wrote a National Register nomination report entitled "The Architectural Legacy of Proudfoot and Bird in Iowa." In Philadelphia, a bastion of Neoclassical architecture, he may also have studied at an atelier called the Square-T Club.

When Proudfoot returned West around 1885, Proudfoot and Bird decided to go to Wichita, then in the throes of a real estate boom driven by the Atchison, Topeka and Santa Fe terminal being located there for the railroad that would serve the West. There they got plenty of work of all kinds, among which was Wichita's city hall, a Richardsonian design of rusticated walls, strong arches and imposing towers at each of the four corners. Curiously, the architects got credit in the press for this commission as Proudfoot and Bird "of Philadelphia." This

The Equitable Insurance Company of Iowa commissioned Proudfoot, Bird and Rawson to affirm the company's importance in Iowa and beyond. *Courtesy of Nelson Construction and Development.*

could have meant that an Eastern pedigree helped them get the job. In any case, the Wichita building is a strong example of a style extremely popular in the 1880s and early '90s for public architecture.

The boom in Wichita slackened by 1890, and after more barnstorming, they joined with a local architect in Salt Lake City to build the City and County Building in the Utah capital. Again, it was a large work of Richardsonian design, though significantly (some said "monstrously") over budget. They returned to Des Moines in 1896 and settled in, with Proudfoot adept at selling the firm's services and Bird regarded as an excellent designer. Early success in Iowa came with the University of Iowa's Schaeffer Hall. Later they won the Engineering Hall at Iowa State, like Schaeffer a Neoclassical work. By then, happily, they were enjoying a reputation for bringing major buildings in on budget. Their success with the Polk County Courthouse put Proudfoot and Bird on a glide path to preeminence locally.

THE COMMERCIAL STYLE IN DES MOINES

In 1913, Proudfoot, Bird and Rawson—as it was then called—designed downtown's Hubbell Building, center of that family's real estate holdings. The ten-story building was significant because it followed the fashion for the simple "commercial style," also identified as the Chicago School, which was introduced in Des Moines by Daniel Burnham's Fleming Building in 1907. The Hubbell Building solidified the firm's relationship with the family, who would bring a series of future commissions, including the family mausoleum and, significantly, a skyscraper to house the Equitable Life Insurance Company of Iowa. In choosing the Proudfoot firm to design the Equitable, the Hubbells and their partners probably expected the latest architectural style, whatever it might be. That would be, the architects said, the Gothic Revival.

One can only speculate how Proudfoot, Bird and Rawson kept up with national trends in urban architecture. Proudfoot appears to have been a book and magazine collector, as their successor firm, Brooks, Borg and Skiles, still has volumes with his name in them. Bird and later Rawson certainly consulted these publications as they designed. However they did it, the firm discerned and adapted without delay to developments in their profession.

Until the Equitable Building, completed in 1924, classical ornament was the most common way to decorate Des Moines' public and commercial buildings. Witness Hotel Fort Des Moines (1913), a Proudfoot building, and the Midland Building (1913), designed by Sawyer and Watrous; both have Chicago School simplicity but are ornamented at base and roofline to recall the nobility of Greece and Rome, not to mention Paris and Chicago's Columbian Exposition.

The lobby of the Equitable Building continues in the Gothic style. *Courtesy of Foutch Brothers LLC.*

But as construction technology (and architectural daring) promised a new age of ever-taller skyscrapers, architects searched for new and more suitable designs for tall buildings. New York's Woolworth Building, an important milestone and the world's tallest structure when built in 1913, was ornamented with Gothic arches and finials that emphasized verticality as classical orders rarely did. Then in 1922 came the Tribune Tower Competition in Chicago. The winning entry by Hood and Howells was distinctly Gothic at the base and high above had ornately Gothic flying buttresses. The effect was an undeniable image of upward thrust. While Tribune Tower as built was well regarded by most, the competition's unbuilt second-place entry by Eliel Saarinen turned out to be even more influential for its modernized but somehow Gothic profile. Saarinen's sleek buttresses ran up the side of each vertical section, dissolving into finials before the next setback section climbed still higher.

The Equitable Building was hardly a version of Saarinen, nor even of Tribune Tower. But the Equitable gave Des Moines a substantial taste of Gothic styling. Ornament at the base was inspired by Gothic buildings typically massive at the ground and lighter, even dissolving, as they went higher. The Equitable's heavy terra-cotta ornament at the base becomes sparser as it ascends through the first several floors and eventually dissolves into plain brick on the building's shaft.

Something of the same thing occurs near the top, with Gothic arches reaching to the roofline, which is a delicate parapet of indeterminate style. There is no sense of imitation here or even slavish following of real Gothic models. And as if to prove its originality, the roofline on its west side is not Gothic at all, rather Neoclassical with urns, swags and Beaux-Arts relief. The penthouse tower on the roof has much the same blend of styles, Gothic and classical, but emphasizing height with a pointed cone roof.

SIXTH AVENUE CANYON

Trends continued to change in the overheated economy of the 1920s, and the Proudfoot firm did not repeat anything like the Equitable. Instead, it moved to something newer still in the Des Moines Building. Here, the designer was likely Harry Rawson, who had joined the firm in 1910 and soon became the design arbiter. Rawson's credentials were good, as he had worked early in his career for J.L. Silsbee in Chicago—Silsbee was a proponent of the Richardsonian and Shingle styles and was the first important employer of Frank Lloyd Wright. When Rawson came home to Des Moines around

The Des Moines Building, the city's largest Art Deco high-rise. *Courtesy of Nelson Construction.*

1900, his politically connected family certainly helped him get commissions, initially in partnership with George Hallett. But talent also helped. The Des Moines Building, completed in 1931, was in a thoroughly up-to-date Art Deco style and remains one of downtown Des Moines' more handsome buildings.

Des Moines architecture suggests that some people in this city dodged the early trials of the Great Depression. They included the Des Moines Building's owner, Arthur Sanford, who had come here from Sioux City. Sanford was an investor in the bond business, which he described, according to his obituary in 1981, as the "marshalling dollars," so as to put them toward useful ends. In Sioux City, he also constructed buildings, which included the Insurance Exchange in 1917. He had others, but the Des Moines Building would be his most ambitious real estate holding to date. Sanford was a good client, said one architect who worked for him previously. Aside from being solvent, "He is a very discerning observer, knows materials and will not accept bad taste or imitation from a designer."

Both Sanford and Rawson understood that the Des Moines Building would be a new centerpiece of the Sixth Avenue Canyon, so-named by the *Register* in 1930 because it was lined by high-rises. Streamlined design was the fashion, driven in many ways by European modernism, also by Saarinen's unbuilt Tribune design. The Des Moines Building's continuous piers rise from a strong granite base to the twelfth story. Two additional stories are set back—the setback being a sleek gesture devised for Manhattan on a larger scale to admit more sunlight into its "canyons."

The flat massing of the Des Moines Building was called Art Deco, something of a misnomer, as *Art Decoratif* from early 1920s France was marked by varied colors, materials and forms. (Art Moderne is more apt for this plain exterior.) But the interior certainly is Art Deco, or at least the lobby, which is where its expensive decoration mostly went. The floor is no ordinary terrazzo but rather "a rich cloisonné of jagged geometric designs with alternating colors of black and speckled gray, accented by the golden lines of brass cloisons separating the patterns." That was how it was put by historian Will Page, who prepared the nominating petition to have the building placed on the National Register of Historic Places in 2013. Polished black marble, bright chrome door frames and elaborate cornices with a chevron pattern are included in the repertoire. It was meant to overwhelm, or at least to defy the Depression, and it did.

The other Art Deco masterpiece of downtown, the Iowa–Des Moines National Bank (later the Valley National and now the U.S. Bank) proved once again that Proudfoot, Rawson, Souers and Thomas, as it was now called, was reshaping downtown. Des Moines was following other cities with streamlined buildings that gave skyscrapers the soaring profile that they desired. The irony was that the bank, which was intended for twenty stories, was completed in 1932 with only five, reduced for economic reasons. Yet the exterior has a sculptural quality even in its truncated state. This demonstrates that Art Deco architecture, like the Gothic, enjoys an intricate and compliant geometry. It can be fashioned into many shapes and sizes.

As for the interior, the bank's marvelous decoration was probably enhanced by the reduced program, which left budget for the ceilings, elevator doors, grilles, banking furniture and, not least, the elaborate decorative safe in the cellar. So many influences are evident in these designs. Besides a love of polished granite and elaborate metalwork (bronze, brass and nickel), the designers were also fascinated by the era's archaeology. The discovery of King Tut's tomb was not too far past, and Egyptian designs show up, along with Aztec, Mayan, Pompeiian and other

Black granite detailing provides a dramatic contrast to limestone walls. *Steve Foritano photograph.*

Metal work became a keynote of Art Deco architecture. *Steve Foritano photograph.*

The banking hall, later of Valley National and ultimately U.S. Bank, lent an air of importance to any transaction. *Courtesy of Knowles Blunck Architecture.*

Gate to the vault. *Steve Foritano photograph.*

patterns from antiquity. It was all stylized to create a visual symphony from the first-floor lobby and up a flight to the double-height banking hall. This became the most elegant interior in downtown Des Moines and made a visit to the bank during hard economic times feel positively fashionable.

FROM FIRE HOUSE TO SOCIAL CLUB

The Proudfoot firm had to feel emboldened by its success in the Iowa–Des Moines National Bank. A subsequent commission, the Des Moines Fire Department Headquarters at Muberry and Ninth, completed in 1938, became even more emphatically modern. Late-model firefighting equipment may also have inspired a design dedicated to streamlined function. On the edge of downtown, the fire department would now have one building for several separate functions: to house firefighters, garage the engines, conduct training and administrate the department.

Before embarking on this one, Proudfoot and company studied state-of-the-art fire station architecture and learned that it increasingly incorporated living quarters and offices. It also had drive-through bays for apparatus. At the same time, fire departments tended to be conservative. "As unexceptional as possible," is how one firefighting historian characterized most firehouse design at the time.

But Des Moines had a confident and powerful chief in William Burnett, who had been with the department since 1895. He had presided over the modernization of the department from the time that stations were essentially barns for horse-drawn fire engines. Whatever happened between Burnett and his architects was exceptional. Proudfoot, Rawson, Brooks and Borg definitely highlighted functionality—minutes could mean lives in this business—with streamlined form most obvious today in the rounded piers between garage doors. Despite some design defects—the piers are too thick and evidently got in the way of the fire engines—when completed, the building was widely praised in the press and by city fathers.

In some ways, the measure of any architecture is in its usefulness over time. While the fire department moved on, the station became suitable for something new: the Des Moines Social Club, a nonprofit arts organization and place for popular dining establishments. While transitions of this kind can hardly be predicted by original architects, certain elements suited to firefighting helped make it a successful arts center. The twenty-first-century architecture firm Slingshot took the clear span space of the garage bays and created an energetic restaurant interior. A large

The old Fire Department building had a multi-use design that now serves as the Des Moines Social Club. *Cameron Campbell photograph.*

courtyard designed for training is now a music venue. The station's ex–repair shop now serves as a theater.

"It has a unity of design that is very difficult when you're building a structure for two different uses…of housing trucks and, second, of housing men. Usually, in a fire station, there's a disunity of design because of two functions. This is an excellent building," wrote the head of the Iowa State architecture department in 1961. The assessment holds true, as the building became an engine in helping to revitalize downtown Des Moines.

Chapter 9

DES MOINES ART CENTER
Expansive Icon

James D. Edmundson never saw the building that his money made possible, but he evidently didn't want to. When the financier died in 1933, he left some $600,000 in securities to the Des Moines Fine Arts Association, which at the time had a small, insignificant space. The bequest would go toward building a proper museum, but it came with the provision that it be held in trust until at least ten years after the donor's death. Edmundson, a self-educated native of Mahaska County, was already an octogenarian when the Great Depression hit the nation. He knew that the waiting period would enable the value of the trust to rise.

Edmundson was right in more ways than one. The time that the arts association was obliged to sit on the money did see the assets grow; it also enabled the beneficiaries to consider how they would spend it. When ready to build, Des Moines had considered and discarded a number of options in terms of site and design. It ultimately decided to create a groundbreaking museum.

The Des Moines Art Center's original building, the first of three major wings, was designed by Eliel Saarinen, completed in 1948. The building, seemingly modest, is a design of great power, so great that it inspired the museum to build a renowned collection to fill it. The Art Center also became the first of many major works of modern architecture in Des Moines, which include new wings to this museum as well as other mid-century masterpieces elsewhere in town.

The museum's success is a triumph but not too surprising, as the founders had serious intentions from an early date. The Fine Arts Association was made up of connoisseurs and enthusiasts whose first quarters were a gallery in the Public Library in 1916. An early success was a 1917 exhibition of three hundred French and Belgian paintings on tour after being on exhibit at the Panama-Pacific Exposition in San Francisco. The arts association was well-supported—by the the Des Moines Women's Club among others—and sometimes filled the library

In the Des Moines Art Center, Eliel Saarinen turned away from needless grandeur and toward forms that would make people comfortable and curious. *Courtesy of Des Moines Art Center.*

The Art Center's exterior shows interest in the craft of building with limestone. *Photography © Cameron Campbell. Courtesy of Des Moines Art Center.*

building with art and crowds large enough to demonstrate that Des Moines was hungry for culture.

In 1940, the association occupied a rented walk-up on Locust Street. The group was not known for avant-garde art, but that year it brought in an auspicious exhibit about the architectural competition for a new art museum for the Smithsonian Institution. Drawings of ten entries were shown, including the winning one by Eliel Saarinen. Some of the projects were conventional and classical, the way museums were expected to be. But Saarinen's was unlike anything that most people had ever seen. It had flat roofs, asymmetrical wings and seemingly thin walls—so untraditional that controversy ensued when it won over the Washington jury. Congress cried that it would not fund such a thing, and it was never built. The National Gallery, a Neoclassical design by John Russell Pope, went up instead in 1941.

The lobby was sleek and well lighted from outside. *Courtesy of Des Moines Art Center.*

The competition exhibit was mounted largely because the association was ready for its museum, but even then there was hardly a groundswell to bring Saarinen to town. At the time, the trustees in charge of the Edmundson fund were mostly focused on the selection of a site that would meet the bequest's condition that it should not be "east of West Fourteenth Street unless the smoke nuisance" that long plagued downtown could be overcome. That phrase left hope for a riverfront location, but trustees eventually concluded that it risked noncompliance. Other possible sites included existing buildings: Terrace Hill, which was doubtful because of conditions of the Hubbell trust, and also Salisbury House, which was in need of a viable tenant. Ultimately, it was determined that the construction of a new building was within reach and that Greenwood Park, on a grassy ridge over Grand Avenue, was the most "sightly location," as the trustees put it.

An agreement to acquire the site from the city was settled by 1941, but it was still unclear what kind of a design would go there. Proudfoot, Rawson, Brooks and Borg, as the city's leading firm was then called, had been hired to do some research, and they toured other museums. The result of that effort was a "very confusing amount of information…from existing museums in other cities," wrote Ding Darling, the cartoonist and civic leader who headed the board.

Clearly, Des Moines wanted something that was practical, useful and would not compete in monumentality with other cities. To get the selection process started, a design scheme was requested from New York architect Eric Gugler, who had recently redesigned the interior of the West Wing of the White House. Gugler, known for staid traditional architecture, presented a design that included an orangery of some sort, but that was considered too extravagant. Memories are that John Brooks of the Proudfoot firm then suggested Saarinen.

Eliel Saarinen was already one of the world's more famous architects. A Finn, he had a European orientation with an interest in new building technologies, much like the Bauhaus. But he was even more attuned to the English Arts and Crafts style (as was Frank Lloyd Wright), which valued simple construction, practical layout and handmade ornament. (Saarinen's unbuilt but influential design for Tribune Tower was not exactly Arts and Crafts, but it was influential for its blend of modern simplicity and warmth drawn from history.) He founded an academy for the "integrated arts" at Cranbrook in Michigan, involving architecture along with painting, sculpture and decorative arts. For the Cranbrook School, he designed distinctive buildings, many in brick and in a comfortable (and now iconic) blend of modern and traditional styles.

It is to Des Moines' credit that the trustees of the foundation ignored the political acrimony that could be thrown at modernism. Whether or not Saarinen's Smithsonian design was inspired by European ideas—Communist or Nazi sympathies were absurdly invoked—Des Moines saw modernism for its most important asset: straightforward utility. The trustees wanted more than exhibit space in their new building. Its designation as an "art center" reflected an early desire that it be a place for education and "an atmosphere of art creation," as Saarinen interpreted his clients' desire. Monumentality was out. A horizontal profile would harmonize with the gentle rise of the site while also suiting Iowans' unpretentious attitude about art and about themselves.

The building is distinctly informal and as different from what might have been expected of a museum as the unbuilt Smithsonian design. Saarinen clearly meant to change the usual sensation of a museum visitor from intimidation to a gentle embrace of the senses. The choice of materials was humble: Lannon limestone quarried mostly in Wisconsin. (It had already been used in the trelliage of the Greenwood Park rose garden.) The building remained low in deference to the site. And the meandering layout was filled with a variety of visual experiences, from intimate galleries to varied views of the landscape outside.

Saarinen's design turned out to be modernism at its best, elegant, functional and, we now see, timeless. The museum seems simple as it sits unobtrusively above Grand

Avenue. Only on closer inspection does a visitor notice exquisite details such as the rough-cut masonry and the courtyard where a reflecting pool shimmers with light that enters the lobby and animates it. Inside are sublime finishes like the plain oak wall panels and polished stone pavements, plus a gentle interior flow that seems natural but is actually an ingenious procession of space. *Architectural Forum* praised the building by saying, "It is a newly emphasized axiom that people will not like art if their feet hurt, or if they are made to feel like schoolchildren on a tour." It requires a building like this to make that otherwise banal observation profound.

THE SUBLIME BRUTALISM OF I.M. PEI

The next section or wing to be built, designed by I.M. Pei and completed in 1968, demonstrates that two styles ostensibly so different can, in skilled hands, fit seamlessly together. Architecture had changed in the twenty years since the first wing, and when Pei designed his part of the museum, the material of choice was not ashlar limestone but rather poured-in-place concrete. The style is, perhaps unfortunately, called "brutalism."

But the result was hardly brutal. New York art critic Emily Genauer wrote at the time that Pei's building represented "a concept which sees architecture as sculpture." Others "remarked that the new building seemed to enhance both the art within, and the existing building beyond," as Iowa State professors Thomas Leslie and Jason Alread recounted in a later article on the building. Pei's building was a triumph when built and remains a milestone of his towering career.

Credit also goes to the clients who understood the basic requirements of the new wing with clarity. For one, it should feature spaces to accommodate the larger scale of contemporary art, especially sculpture and installations. At the same time, the addition would not overwhelm or compete with the Saarinen building. In fact, Saarinen's firm in Michigan (both Eliel and his son Eero were dead by this time) was contacted, but they were too busy to consider the commission. Trustees then sought another "well-known non-local architect," as they put it. They found Pei, who later said that he understood the assignment as "to reconcile two generations of architecture without compromising either, so that one plus one would equal more than two."

Pei, Chinese born and Harvard educated, was not then the luminary that he later became, especially in museum design. His modernist East Wing of the National Gallery would come later, as did his glass pyramid in the courtyard of the Louvre. But he had shown himself to be an artist in the material of reinforced concrete with such buildings as the National Center for Atmospheric Research in Boulder. In that one, he mediated between the geological strength of Brutalism and its capacity for articulate,

I.M. Pei's so-called brutalist Art Center wing in Greenwood Park. *Photography © Cameron Campbell. Courtesy of Des Moines Art Center.*

Pei brought his 1968 addition to the edge of the reflecting pool designed by Saarinen but preserved the view of the park through the wing's open interior space. *Courtesy of Des Moines Art Center.*

even delicate geometry. As for all of Des Moines' requirements, Pei understood. When trustee David Kruidenier, Art Center trustee and publisher of the *Register*, had an initial meeting with the architect, Pei took out a piece of tracing paper and sketched a plan and elevation so well thought out "that the sheer act of creativity left me breathless," Kruidenier said.

The Pei addition remains downslope behind the Saarinen building and is almost invisible from Grand Avenue. At the same time, it provides a double- (even triple-) height exhibition space where large works of sculpture have room and natural illumination. As for light, the butterfly-shape of the skylight (the only part of the building visible from in front of the Art Center) provides abundantly from above. While the strength of the concrete walls is imposing, it is pierced with large windows that not only illuminate the interior but also provide a view from the courtyard, now enclosed, through to the rose garden. Saarinen's subtle axis is preserved.

RICHARD MEIER'S GEOMETRIC PUZZLE

Little more than a decade later, yet another wing was needed. Trustees returned to their previous architect, but Pei declined in what seemed like another gesture of deference to the building's signature architect, Saarinen. Yet the trustees were confident that their museum represented an attractive commission, so they developed a list of five major architects. They told each that the Art Center's third wing would have three main elements: gallery space, a café and a service wing (with loading dock).

The competitors were invited to Des Moines to make their presentations, and when Meier made his, he spoke for most of his allotted forty minutes with the model of his design-entry covered. Recollections are that he talked about the many requirements of this important building, and still without revealing his design, he verbally explained how he met them.

Then he pulled the sheet off. Naturally, the committee was eager to reconcile the model with what Meier had made them imagine. Both Meier and the trustees succeeded, evidently, as the model looked very much like what was built: a white, porcelainized metal composition of curves and straight lines. It looked so unlike the previous wings, but so had the Pei seemed different from the Saarinen.

Meier was a member of a group of the New York Five, architects who were classed together by critics for their interest in the geometry of space. As they invoked predecessors like Corbusier, they appeared more concerned with the subjective elements of architecture such as light and perception than with structure. One could also describe Meier as an "intellectual" architect of ideas, rather than an organic one grounded in physics and nature. Perhaps this—the

The Richard Meier wing of the museum. *Courtesy of Des Moines Art Center.*

intellect or some brand of obscure logic—was how the trustees reckoned that they might link the two existing wings, themselves connected by an almost spiritual marriage, with a third.

Meier's most physical link between the Saarinen and the Pei is, curiously, social—a social space. It is the café, positioned in the corner of the courtyard, which is the one place where the three architects' works are simultaneously visible. The white-clad café has a deceptive harmony with the older two phases, perhaps because one sees little of its exterior from the windows.

But harmony with what existed previously is not Meier's main objective (though the exterior has a definite similarity to Des Moines' mid-century icon, the Butler Mansion). In the gallery space of the new wing, an atrium connects three levels and a skylight with a geometric puzzle that appears to float and creates endless curiosity by suggesting circles and squares and then letting the spatial geometry dissolve at the edges. White walls, light wooden floors, sunlight from skylight and glass walls and a winding staircase comprise as much a work of abstract art as some of the sculpture and paintings that it contains.

The one thing everyone notices about the Meier wing is that it has none of the restraint that characterizes the previous two. To some, it disappoints, but it remains a significant sign of its time. The year before his new Art Center wing was opened, Meier won the 1984 Pritzker Prize, the so-called Nobel Prize of architecture. That recognition came when postmodernism, sentimentalized reworkings of history, was

Meier's intricate geometry outside foreshadows the spaces within. *Courtesy of Des Moines Art Center.*

The galleries seek to enrich the art-viewing experience from above and below. *Courtesy of Des Moines Art Center.*

The building seems to exist in a near-colorless realm where art comes quickly alive. *Courtesy of Des Moines Art Center.*

the profession's fashion. Meier and others of the New York Five largely rejected that trend and reasserted the spatial principles of modernism.

At the same time, the Art Center was increasingly renowned for its collection, not vast but of high quality. Its *Automat* had become one of Edward Hopper's more famous pictures, so much so that it would make the cover of *Time*. Francis Bacon's *Portrait of Pope Innocent* has been featured in a popular BBC documentary. Other works proved that the Des Moines Art Center had achieved a stature that few Iowans might have anticipated when they asked Eliel Saarinen to town. By the third wing's 1985 opening, the museum was an institution of national repute. Richard Meier did nothing to hide that proud fact.

Chapter 10

MODERNISM AT DRAKE

E liel Saarinen taught that architects should design with an eye on "the next larger thing" as a way to achieve harmony with the natural or built environment. This idea led to the Art Center's rapport with its site on Greenwood Park. It was this sense of scale and unity that also impressed Henry G. Harmon, president of Drake University, when it was on the verge of significant expansion on its antique campus on University Avenue.

After World War II, Drake's enrollment exploded, doubling to more than six thousand, a great many of them veterans returning from service. Drake was short of dormitories at the time—with most students living off campus—and also in need of modern classrooms. "Drake can be one of the fine, middle-sized universities of the Midwest, or it can be a much smaller school, serving primarily the youth of Des Moines," Harmon wrote to the trustees in 1948. In fact, the die had been cast. Enrollment was not likely to shrink, and Harmon had already engaged Saarinen to plan a much larger campus.

Saarinen brought modern ideas about planning as well as architecture. As in his design buildings, good planning often meant asymmetry, which acknowledged that function should overshadow form. "One instructive way to understand the significance of Drake's decision to build in the modern style is to examine the stylistic path that it did not choose," wrote Maura Lyons of the Drake art history department in a 2008 monograph on the campus. What they discarded was a traditional plan drawn in 1943 or thereabouts featuring symmetrical quadrangles with buildings big and small occupying predictable positions. The architectural style was Georgian, prompted by the stately new library recently built when those quads were proposed.

If Saarinen saw this plan, his view of it would have been predictably negative. It was not because he disliked Georgian architecture. It was because it had little to do with Drake's future needs. He would have said, one can surmise, that it was imitative and based on ideas evolved elsewhere, perhaps at the famous University of Virginia designed by Thomas Jefferson.

Saarinen knew that college campuses were like organisms that would grow over time according to unknowable future influences. When he discussed planning, Saarinen often cited medieval cities, which grew by many hands across centuries. He was not planning quite that far in the future for Drake—quite the contrary—but he knew that even the short-term future would make a strictly classical plan either futile or counterproductive. Instead he laid out trapezoidal greens, which, Maura Lyons points out, resemble something medieval, especially Piazza San Marco in Venice, which Saarinen called "a lasting symphony of architectural form, just because of its many and well-balanced styles."

Eliel Saarinen's plan for Drake was not followed with precision, as plans rarely are. But it did inspire two major axes, one crossing the other. And instead of a monument or fountain at dead center, the plan and actual campus have clusters of buildings that represent multiple focal points of the campus, not a single one. This was the modernist approach and might have seemed radical in theory. In practice, it enabled harmony with the past. As son Eero Saarinen went on to design nine buildings at Drake—with an eye to his father's plan—none of them looked anything like the largest building on campus, Old Main. Nevertheless, that big Victorian structure was given its space at the edge of the main lateral axis, plus its power to influence buildings that went up around it.

"It was at Drake University where a new age of modern architecture began," said architect Philip Johnson not too many years later. That was hyperbole, perhaps, but the story is a pioneering one. Drake's move toward modernism began, President Harmon said, with a letter from a stranger who had seen the proposed classical plan for Drake and complained that it represented "the architecture of the past for the students of the future." Harmon's interest in advanced architecture was reinforced by his visit to Cranbrook School in Michigan, where the Saarinens, father and son, lived and designed a mostly Arts and Crafts–style campus.

In fact, Eero Saarinen's new architecture for the Drake campus is not Arts and Crafts. Instead, it is tempting to cite his design for the General Motors Technical Center in Bloomfield Hills, Michigan, as an antecedent for Drake. The GM Center is sprawling and integrated while also serving varied functions. Like GM, Drake features plain modern buildings that emphasize space, inside and out, and not ornament. Of course, Drake is not GM, and despite similarities, the differences between the two places may be even more revealing.

While GM was built from the ground up on a blank slate, the Drake buildings became part of an existing campus and would have failed entirely if they had clashed with what was already there. Drake had traditional roots, architecturally. And while heavy, picturesque structures were exactly what Saarinen was not going to do, he

Old Main at Drake shared little with modern architecture except for brick, the material that remained a keynote of the campus. *Courtesy of Special Collections, Cowles Library, Drake University.*

found other ways to harmonize with "the next larger thing." Brick was an element of the existing environment and could be used in the new. Designs of low profile were a way to harmonize with the low roll of the campus's terrain.

Ingham Hall of Science and Fitch Hall of Pharmacy, complete in 1949, were the first Saarinen buildings to go up. Their designs are as straightforward as their reasons for being built, which were that World War II had foreshadowed the importance of science in the twentieth century. As for the architecture, Saarinen believed that polemics between modern and traditional design had been long settled in favor of the former. Accordingly, it meant that these buildings would be eloquent only to the extent that their forms followed their functions. Saarinen used subtle notes of the old architecture in the stone base and brick end walls. But more essential to the architecture were window walls with insulated spandrels developed by metal-working engineers at Chrysler. If the building parts were prosaic, however, they set themselves apart by the precision and sense of proportion in the way they were assembled. This was Saarinen's touchstone.

An example of this attribute exists in the lecture halls at the end of Ingham. They are enclosed by a curved brick wall, organically shaped and sculptural, containing spaces where the function inside is evermore important than any ornament that might decorate the outside. The shape derives from two separate halls of unequal size fit together so that they might share audio-visual devices (such as they were). Another note of "form follows function" was a bridge between Ingham to Fitch, emphasizing

Outside the auditorium at
Harvey Ingham Hall, a building
that helped change the curve of
college architecture. *Courtesy of
Special Collections, Cowles Library,
Drake University.*

Fitch Hall of Pharmacy was no
less modern for its limestone
base and brick end wall, nor
out of place on an old campus.
*Courtesy of Special Collections,
Cowles Library, Drake University.*

Two lecture halls of different sizes share one ample foyer. *Courtesy of Special Collections, Cowles Library, Drake University.*

A stairway to the bridge between two buildings provides an open place where students can meet. *Courtesy of Special Collections, Cowles Library, Drake University.*

the connection between the sciences and pharmacy. The bridge emanates from a glass entry in Ingham with a "floating" steel stairway within. The composition more than satisfies the modernist quest for universal space that dissolves walls and justifies minimalism to embrace what is beyond the confines of the single building.

"COST TO A MINIMUM" IN THE QUADRANGLE DORMS

After Ingham and Fitch were built, the important *Progressive Architecture* magazine praised the buildings in no uncertain terms. "We present these buildings as remarkably successful and beautiful examples of integrated design. We also consider it even more remarkable that an established institution of higher learning would commission and accept such unpretentious architecture." So much for Saarinen's aesthetic credentials. But his next project for Drake would test his ability to face the sometimes onerous economy that modern architecture was also expected to address. The project was a cluster of new dormitories.

Harmon wrote to Saarinen as they embarked on this step: "We must make compromises with the desirable to hold building cost to a minimum." Up to the

In Eero Saarinen's hands simple forms created interest and even drama. *Danny Akright photograph. Courtesy of Drake University.*

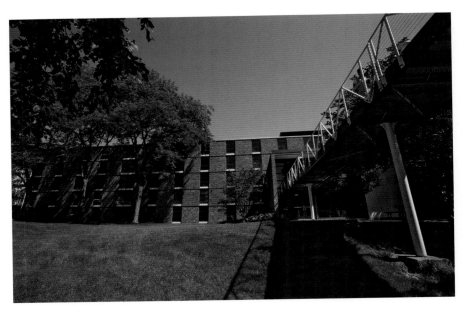

Bridges connect the four dorms of the Quadrangle with the dining hall. *Danny Akright photograph. Courtesy of Drake University.*

task, Saarinen researched the problem until he had a conversation with a structural engineer who worked with him on the St. Louis Arch competition. Together they devised a system of precast concrete slabs, faced in brick and assembled on a concrete frame "like a house of cards," it was said.

In each of four dormitories, Saarinen made a virtue of necessity with an exceedingly simple, repetitious design. Each brick slab corresponds to a dorm room, which inspired exteriors of clean geometric interest. What is more distinctive, even ingenious, is the way the dorms and a dining hall are sited around a gentle ravine. Saarinen put a reflecting pool at the bottom of the basin, giving the buildings a visual unity (the pool was later reconfigured into a kind of stony creek). Tying them together are pedestrian bridges, also minimal but very long with thin metal rails. These bridges connect to the dorms at double-height commons rooms, each with a balcony inside that heightens the theatricality of places where people are apt to meet.

The Hubbell Dining Hall, shared by all students living in the Quadrangle Dormitories, was not quite so constrained by a minimal budget. It has a more dynamic profile than the dorms—the horizontal mass of the building appears to slide over the slope of its site, undergirded on its low end with a brick-clad ground floor. Above, the building has a mildly Cubist air with floor-to-ceiling limestone panels and glass walls. The glass is recessed, which admits more natural light than otherwise and also provides larger views from outside of what is within: a large open space.

The Hubbell Dining Hall displays its open interior from the distance outside. *Danny Akright photograph. Courtesy of Drake University.*

The Stuart Davis mural *Allée* was later moved to a less vulnerable place in the student union. *Courtesy of Special Collections, Cowles Library, Drake University.*

The dining hall was distinguished enough for the Gardner Cowles Foundation, of the family that owned the *Des Moines Register*, to finance American artist Stuart Davis to create a colorful abstract work that remains a treasure of the university. Of his first visit to the building, Davis said, "I remembered the whiteness of the room—its ceiling and walls—the black floors, the blue sky outside those windows, and the red rectangles of the brick dormitories." It inspired a composition of form and color entitled *Allée* (which was later moved to the student union due to the risk of a priceless painting in a place where students dine).

When the Quadrangle Dormitories were completed in 1951, there was enthusiasm even among those not yet devoted to the modernist ideal. "If a student lives in this atmosphere for four years…he should emerge with a new appreciation of beauty which should entitle him to a degree in liberal arts even though he never attends a class or opens a book," wrote a reporter from the *Register* shortly after the buildings were completed. Exaggeration or not, it was a sign that Saarinen and his client had succeeded in applying modernism without incurring the wrath of a public with normally traditional tastes.

SAARINEN'S CHAPEL: SPIRITUALITY AND MODESTY

Perhaps Saarinen's most interesting quality as an architect, from a distance of more than fifty years, would be unpredictability. In his own time, critics struggled to understand if modern architecture was strictly minimalist or represented the embrace of unique and surprising designs. Saarinen did nothing to resolve the question when he undertook two buildings for the Drake Divinity School. One of them, Medbury Hall, was essentially as minimalist as his science buildings and dormitories. With the adjacent Oreon E. Scott Chapel, the architect and his partners did something almost totally unexpected in creating a tiny and deeply expressive place.

As a classroom building for Drake's "bible school," Medbury fit into the aesthetic of brick, glass and metal that had been successful in Ingham and Fitch, though Medbury is smaller and has a proportionately tighter pattern in the glass wall. Despite changes over the years—today's bronzed wall panels are different from the porcelainized metal that Saarinen designed—it retains the Cubist profile and glassiness that is striking on the lawn in the middle of campus.

What makes Medbury special, of course, is its neighbor, the chapel, to which it is connected by a canopy. In a sense, the chapel's exterior is as simple as the glass box next door—a brick cylinder or "drum" without windows. But even on the outside, the architect signals that the plain is not ordinary. The wall has texture with a pattern of recessed bricks all around. But its true singularity begins when the visitor enters the

Medbury Hall and the Scott Chapel, built for the Divinity School, show that great architecture need not call attention to itself. *Courtesy of Substance Architecture.*

dark interior, a round space with seats and standing room for forty or fifty worshippers at the most. Even before eyes become accustomed to the dark, a round travertine table in the middle becomes visible, bathed in natural light from a heptagonal skylight. If people are present, they are seated in twenty high-backed oak chairs behind a circular rail. The design is unfamiliar, truly restful and meant to be spiritual.

The simplicity and size of the chapel were enforced by the university's condition: "minimum of finances and maximum need." But the result was fortuitous. The transcendent aspect of sunlight on plain table is hardly extravagant, but the subtle grain of the stone fixes the eye on something primeval. Dr. John McCaw, then dean of the Divinity School, remembered that an underground chapel had been imagined by the architects before it was deemed far too expensive.

Whether awe and mystery were foremost in the minds of McCaw and Saarinen as the building was designed, it also corresponds to other specific ideas about the school's denomination, the Disciples of Christ. McCaw explained to Saarinen the importance of a circle, that it had spiritual significance in almost every religious tradition. Beyond that, the circle also expressed the democratic nature of the Disciples of Christ. And McCaw still thinks of the travertine table as a communion table and not an altar. "I wanted to make sure that we were not emphasizing [the pastor's] ego," said McCaw whose mission it was to train ministers.

For a structure that could evoke such spirituality, Saarinen designed a flat ceiling of seven exposed beams coming together at the skylight. Within that, seven

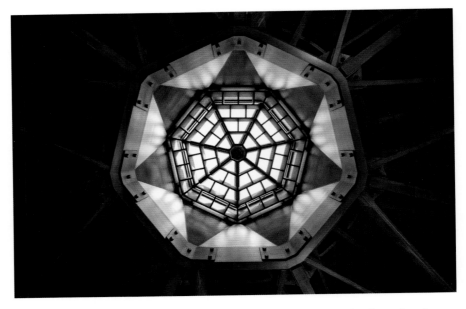

The Scott Chapel skylight, restored in 2006 by Substance Architecture, has facets that change the direction and quality of light as the sun passes overhead. *Courtesy of Substance Architecture.*

corresponding panels of glass diffuse light in various ways at different times of day. "It was an incredibly ingenious design," said Paul Mankins, of the Des Moines firm Substance Architecture, which restored the chapel in 2006. McCaw said that the shafts of light often heightened the spiritual sensation of the space. The Scott Chapel remains among Saarinen's most important religious structures and a true landmark of mid-century modern architecture.

LESS IS MORE FOR THE SCHOOL OF JOURNALISM

It was simplicity that made an icon of another modernist building on campus, this one by Ludwig Mies van der Rohe. Meredith Memorial Hall was built for the School of Journalism, and there was talk of having Saarinen design it as well. Saarinen declined, he said, because he insisted on his personal involvement in each commission of his office, and he was far too busy.

So in 1958 when Drake was ready to start on Meredith, the university interviewed a number of prominent architects hoping for the same success that it felt that it had with Saarinen. Philip Johnson, Paul Rudolph and Louis Kahn were on the list, but Drake chose Mies largely because of the architect's recent experience in designing an entirely new campus at the Illinois Institute of Technology in Chicago. It was Mies who said, "Less is more." It was he who perfected modern buildings of glass and steel through his almost transcendent understanding of proportion and care in assembling the few and essential parts.

Mies's earliest exposure to architecture came as he was the son of a stone mason in Germany. Other influences reached to nineteenth-century architect Karl Friedrich Schinkel, who designed simplified classical monuments such as the Altes Museum in Berlin (1830), and Hendrik Petrus Berlage, who applied the simplest forms possible, often medieval in character, to functional buildings like factories. Berlage was an early employer of Mies in the Netherlands.

Mies grew in his profession, but the post–World War I years in Germany provided little work for architects. Consequently, he and other ambitious architects occupied themselves in theoretical pursuits. As the trend was toward minimalism, Mies took an interest in the de Stijl movement, which reduced form to linear patterns. He was interested in the Cubists, who redefined space and time, and Mies thought he could do the same with architecture. He also grafted ancient Christianity on these ideas; he read St. Thomas Aquinas, who perceived a spiritual essence in all physical objects.

Perfect proportion makes Meredith Hall appear somehow as a natural part of the landscape. *Courtesy of Drake University.*

This influence is often cited to explain why the architect exposed and even seemed to venerate things as basic as structural steel that other architects usually hid.

Meredith is in some ways a formulaic building, with mullions made of I-beams with floor-to-ceiling panels of spandrels and glass fit perfectly into the openings. Even inside, the simple but ingenious solution of raking two auditoriums back to back had been used by Mies and his office before. What is remarkable about the building, as with so many others of the architect, is that its beauty is in its precision and craftsmanship. The columns at twenty-two-foot intervals correspond to the size of the spaces within. The way the wall panels are inserted into the sills was a subject of much consideration as to how to get the proper grooves fabricated.

For people occupying the building, Meredith Hall induces a sense of repose and peacefulness, not least because of views to the outside. Mies intended to dissolve the divisions between inside and out. As for the exterior, the black-painted steel and tinted glass is almost too simple to be sculptural. Yet it seems today, as when built, an almost natural part of the landscape.

Chapter 11

AN URBAN CAMPUS
FOR FINANCE

It would be hard to select a building that had a greater impact on downtown Des Moines than the Banker's Life Building. This massive Art Deco structure remains a landmark, and one can only imagine its monumental presence before a complex of other buildings for Principal Financial (successor to Banker's Life) grew up around it. The design was lauded in 1940 by *Architectural Record* as one of the nation's most important business buildings since the Depression.

A decade before, Equitable Life Insurance of Iowa had shown that architecture could raise an insurance company's profile while also consolidating its operations. If these benefits were not entirely obvious, Banker's Life president Gerard Nollen may have gotten the message from his brother, Henry Nollen, president of Equitable. Both were conservative and not given to extravagance, which is testimony that large steel framed buildings for growing companies made economic sense.

The Nollens were born in Pella, where their grandfather was a founder of the town of Dutch Reformed immigrants. Father was a banker from whom the boys inherited their mathematical skills, if not the family's religious doctrine. (In Des Moines, the brothers would join more liberal churches.) They were home schooled in Pella, as the Nollens believed that public education hardly equaled what forebearers had had in Europe. Gerard graduated from Grinnell in 1902 and then studied advanced mathematics at Drake. He landed at Banker's Life in 1912.

When Nollen became Banker's Life president in 1926, the company already was selling nationally, initially life policies to bank employees. The company expanded with direct mail marketing, and for a while during Nollen's tenure it owned and advertised on the high-power radio station WHO. Banker's Life was hit by the Depression when many policyholders were forced to allow their coverage to lapse. But conservative management and new products enabled the company to grow, if only slowly, through most of the 1930s.

Banker's Life Building demonstrated once again that insurance companies were serious about architecture. *Photograph © Principal Financial Services, Inc. Used by permission.*

Gerard Nollen's taste for architecture must have been inspired not just by his brother's Equitable Building but also by his wife's family, the Witmers, who were large landowners on the West Side of the city. One of their farms, named Owl's Head, was subdivided as early as the 1890s for fashionable new homes, and the Nollens lived in a house at 2900 Grand Avenue that had been the Witmers'. That fine Georgian mansion was designed by Liebbe, Nourse and Rasmussen, and it later housed the governor of Iowa before Terrace Hill was refitted to that purpose.

What the Banker Life Building signified when completed in 1939 was that the company was looking forward. The Equitable Building, completed in 1924, had touched on the Gothic styling considered advanced for urban high-rises at that time. Now, Banker's Life took its cue from the Art Deco style, even more modern. In this it was following the Des Moines Building and the Iowa–Des Moines National Bank with the vertical thrust of unornamented limestone buttresses, the leitmotif of American cities in the late 1920s and '30s.

The architect of Banker's Life was the firm of Tinsley, McBroom and Higgins of Des Moines, which had never done anything nearly as large. But the partners understood that the insurance business, to be successful, required significant size and an "assembly line" of clerical functions. Architecturally, this meant large floor plates and thoughtful interior plans. "A case in point is the adjacent placement of the actuarial and investment departments on the fifth floor," wrote *Architectural Record*. "Wherever possible, departments with different seasonable peaks have been paired on the same floor. Thus when one is

Streamlined flow was the message of Banker's Life, inside its building and out. *Photograph © Principal Financial Services, Inc. Used by permission.*

having its 'off' season and the other, its busiest, the latter simply expands its work area into that of the former and vice versa."

Perfect flexibility was perhaps more an ideal than reality, but the architects did accomplish "the easiest possible flow of people, things and ideas," as the magazine said. The massive building was large enough for wide hallways and large vestibules, and these inspired a rich display of true Art Deco decor: polished travertine on the walls and sleek metalwork in many details. Its beauty was not merely skin deep; the building was designed for the most modern "atmospheric control" with variable warming and cooling through copper pipes and forced air through perforated ceilings.

As the architects and clients spared no effort in acoustical, electrical and other functional elements, they also dedicated time and treasure in creating art on the walls. Lowell Houser, a friend of Grant Wood and colleague of the Stone City Art Colony, was the lead artist for a variety of works in glass and stone. Themes reached back to Native American history and also to the Mayans, whose ruins were being discovered when the building was going up. Scenes depict the development of corn, a strong connection between Iowa and ancient America. The social realism of the Stone City style, an artistic reaction against European abstraction, still stands the test of time for a company and industry that values clarity.

ORGANIZATION MAN'S ARCHITECT IN DES MOINES

One might not expect that the insurance industry would be on the vanguard of modern architecture. Yet the industry is so tied to efficiency that it became a worthwhile challenge for mid-century modernists to design their buildings. Just as the Banker's Life Building, now the Principal's "Corporate One," became such a building at the end of the Depression, the nearby American Republic headquarters represents another example from a generation later.

American Republic's president Watson Powell Jr. was not purely efficiency-minded when he commissioned this radical office building. Powell was second generation in the business, having been handed the mutual company by his father in 1960. Almost instantly, he began to modernize. For one, the company had been operating in leased spaces in downtown Des Moines, and Powell knew he had to consolidate in a single building. In doing so, American Republic got a cutting-edge work of architecture, completed in 1965, which the president also filled with art bought from the leading artists of the era, including Warhol and Calder. Within a very few years, the company's building and art merited a feature in *Life* magazine.

Powell's architects were from Skidmore Owings and Merrill (SOM), which by the 1950s had become the firm most associated with *The Organization Man*, the popular book

American Republic Insurance was a striking example of a modern corporate headquarters for the corporation now called American Enterprise. *Courtesy of American Republic Insurance.*

and ethos that stressed convention and efficiency above all else. This meant that SOM studied the conditions of any new architectural client exhaustively and objectively before designing and perhaps unexpectedly came up with some of architecture's most innovative designs. Better than any other firm, SOM translated Corbusier's notion, "A house is a machine for living," to commerce.

Nearly a decade before, SOM partner Gordon Bunshaft designed one of the era's first "corporate campus" office buildings for Connecticut General Insurance. That glassy complex outside Hartford was based on Bunshaft's insight—not too different from the Banker's Life program—that "the issue and servicing of an insurance policy bears many resemblances to an assembly line operation in a factory." Connecticut General had plenty of land and got a sprawling low-rise facility, or "a sweeping horizontal motion…the work does not want to go upstairs," as Bunshaft put it.

Republic's Powell invited Bunshaft to visit Des Moines. They came to terms and together considered, then rejected, a "rural" site on Fleur Avenue; Powell said that his clerical workforce mostly lived close to downtown. When they settled on the Sixth Avenue site, Powell probably thought that he would get a "stock" SOM high-rise with glass curtain walls, perhaps like Bunshaft's design for Lever House in New York. But the architect had another idea. His objective was clear-span space with each floor absolutely free of interior supporting columns. This would provide freedom to rearrange functions and furniture as needed.

One senses that the building's innovative design suited SOM's objectives somewhat more than the company's. For some time, SOM architects had been working closely with structural engineers to produce the broadest clear-span spaces possible. Reinforced concrete represented a successful approach to the goal, and Bunshaft proposed to Watson Powell such a building of six floors above grade, forty feet by sixty feet each, absent of interior columns. It would have floor-to-ceiling windows on the short sides, north and south. The east and west walls would be windowless, thus limiting views outside and "distraction." The interiors would be uncluttered in the extreme—desks uniform and knickknacks of any kind discouraged. "The people themselves become the most important feature, the decoration" of the architecture, Powell said in the *Life* magazine article.

While the building seems plain (if outlandish—it is compared to a giant file cabinet), it features details that are endlessly interesting. The concrete walls were sandblasted to expose the granite chips that make the concrete appear not cast but somehow cut from the earth. Each side was constructed on four giant steel hinges, which clearly emphasize the weight of the building and the precision of its construction. While the hinges are dramatic, they do not stray from function, as they allow four sections of each wall to shift independently and avoid cracking. (Powell had visited Eero Saarinen's Dulles Airport outside Washington, D.C., where the concrete structure suffered cracks early in its life.)

The building rests on giant hinges, which raise its distinctive form above the ground and also curtail cracking in concrete walls. *Mark Jongman photograph. Courtesy of American Republic Insurance.*

Art has been a part of the American Republic Building since it opened in 1965. Here is a work by Arnaldo Pomodoro, *Sphere Within a Sphere*, 1999. *Mark Jongman photograph, Courtesy of American Republic Insurance.*

Opposite, bottom: Clear span open space inside creates a distinctive work environment. *Mark Jongman photograph. Courtesy of American Republic Insurance.*

The American Republic interior has a starkness to it—with precast T-beams and exposed utility ducts overhead—but it was emphatically refined with modern art. Bunshaft didn't talk much about the paintings and sculpture in his buildings, though his Chase Manhattan Bank building became known for the stellar collection that it housed. Likewise, the American Republic collection became identified with Powell. He bought a Calder sculpture that graced the courtyard for years. The long, otherwise blank walls inside had Frankenthaler, Lichtenstein, Chermayeff and other names that grew in fame (and value).

Art changed the chairman's life as it changed the lives of the people who worked amid it, mostly for the better. One purchase was not a unanimous triumph, however. That was a commission that went to Andy Warhol, *American Male*, a silkscreened photo of Powell's father repeated thirty-two times, one for every year of his service to the company. The son called it mesmerizing. Watson Powell Sr. hated it so much that it tainted filial ties until the father died. It hung in the building for years but was eventually sold, partly because of its history but also because of its value. But the Warhol story was a small glitch in American Republic's commitment to modernism. "The increase in efficiency is terrific," said Powell, who died in 2000, of his building.

"A PROUD AND SOARING THING"

As Des Moines insurance companies had for decades stamped their success with buildings, a major turning point in sheer scale was triggered in the 1970s when Congress passed ERISA, which enabled the industry to offer a wide range of group pension and retirement products. Banker's Life became aggressive in the area, and with that business, plus a massive book of adjustable premium life business, the company entered a new and highly profitable period. One result in 1985 was a new name, Principal Financial Group. Another, in 1991, was a new address, this time with a skyscraper that would visibly herald the company from well beyond downtown Des Moines.

It was a sign of the company's resolve, as well as its wealth, that when it required a new building, it focused on only one architect, a famous one, from the beginning. Gyo Obata was a partner with the firm Hellmuth, Obata and Kassabaum, later HOK. Headquartered in St. Louis, HOK was known for daringly modern forms, such as the National Air and Space Museum in Washington and Levi's Plaza in San Francisco. It would grow to become one of the largest architecture firms in the world, which it accomplished by being attuned to fashion as much as innovation.

By the 1980s, postmodernism was creating elaborate and sometimes peculiarly formed buildings for corporate America, often with touches of history in massing or detail. Reflecting the boredom that many felt with box-like office buildings, postmodernism became a free-form style, often with arches, columns, pediments and other non-structural additions. Confirmed modernists were suspicious that postmodernism was decorative without substance, and the style ignited debate, especially when Philip Johnson's design for AT&T Tower (1984) in New York went up with its famous "Chippendale" top. Johnson was challenged for being frivolous. He defended himself by calling himself a functionalist, the function in this case being to elicit delight that had been lacking of late.

The Principal's 801 Grand has a postmodern quality, but it is also functional. Its three-level atrium has a dramatic Art Deco feel but is also configured to connect the building to the city's Skywalk system, which had become an integral part of downtown Des Moines. The shaft of the building rises straight up for most of its forty-five stories, with a bulk to provide large floor areas suitable for clerical functions. Some two-thirds

801 Grand changed the scale of Des Moines as its owner, Principal Financial, did the same to the city's insurance industry. *Photograph © Principal Financial Services, Inc. Used by permission.*

The three-story lobby recalls luxury once essential in urban skyscrapers. *Photograph ©
Principal Financial Services, Inc. Used by permission.*

of the way up, the building has shallow setbacks—a note of nostalgia, perhaps, for
the skyscrapers of Manhattan and also for Des Moines' Sixth Avenue Canyon. In the
upper reaches, the profile becomes more complex with rotated squares, a geometry
that is decorative but also utilitarian as it maximizes premium corner office space.

Of course, the building has the ultimate mark of postmodernism, which is
extravagance, especially in the granite cladding that gives the building (and the
company) the look of solidity as well as nostalgia for the time when skyscrapers all
had sheer masonry walls. There was no attempt to utilize local stone for economy or
sustainability. Obata chose Brazilian granite for its warm pinkish color, as opposed to
a colder, grayer domestic granite that might have been used (something like that on
the base of Corporate One).

Lastly, "801" has a copper roof that highlights the taper at the very top of the
skyscraper. Its form—cone-shaped with pleated facets—refers abstractly to the tower

atop the Equitable Building. More importantly, it points skyward and appears a "proud and soaring thing," as called for in skyscrapers by the prophet of modern architecture, Louis Sullivan. The design recalls a time when skyscrapers changed America. This one, driven by a similar impulse, certainly changed Des Moines with its size and grandeur.

CORPORATE FOUR: THE Z BUILDING

At the time that Principal's Z Building, also known as Corporate Four, was imagined, the company had a certain power and confidence. It had become nationally known in areas such as pension management. It had a substantial corporate art collection. So

The Z Building was designed by Helmut Jahn, who was sometimes called the "Flash Gordon of architecture." *Rainer Viertlboeck photograph. Courtesy of Jahn.*

when it was ready to build yet again in the early 1990s, it naturally sought a prominent modern architect. The company quickly came to terms with Helmut Jahn, of the Chicago firm of Murphy Jahn, and began with the sure knowledge that it would get a distinctive if not outlandish design. It did. The Z Building was named, or nicknamed, because its footprint is an outline of the letter—or perhaps it's a thunderbolt—across an oversized city block north of the original Banker's Life.

Jahn was midway in a brilliant career when he arrived in Des Moines, and he cultivated an image to match. When Principal real estate director Randy Manear picked the architect up at the airport for his first visit, Jahn looked every bit like he had been pictured on the cover of *GQ* in 1985. The magazine had written of his fearless architecture and also of his wardrobe. As he got off the plane, he did not disappoint, wearing a cape and fedora hat, escorted by Manear, who admitted that he was dressed like an insurance executive.

It may be that Jahn was in a transitional phase when he arrived in Des Moines. He was already known for a brand of postmodernism, as evidenced by One Liberty Place in Philadelphia, which dominated the skyline with a glassy version of the Chrysler Building. Before that, he had created an abstract dome in the middle of Chicago's Loop for the State of Illinois Building. But by this time, the mid-1990s, postmodernism was out of fashion and Jahn was interested in architecture that emphasized engineering and innovative structure.

Jahn was also entering a more collaborative phase; he was less the master builder and more a member of a team that he would assemble. "We used to do everything ourselves," Jahn said of his practice around this time. For the Principal commission, one critical partner was landscape architect Peter Walker of California. Jahn had already imagined something of a Z form when Walker came on to design a site to tie the company's existing buildings to the new one. The triangular plaza (bearing in mind that the triangle is a part of the Principal's logo) creates diagonal axes across space between buildings, tracing approaches from Principal's Corporate One and Corporate Two. The geometry of the design is meant to attract people into the public space; pavements, stone benches and gardens make the place pleasant to sit in.

An asset of the Z Building is that it positively extended the downtown area and created a plaza in a city that long lacked active street life. "It is very, very public, and it powerfully draws you in," said the American Society of Landscape Architects jury when it recognized the project with a design award in 1998. It was an honor for Walker but also a credit to Jahn and his willingness to share the commission with other artists who brought varied ideas and approaches.

Somewhat after the design of the plaza and the Z Building was settled, Principal took yet another step and invited sculptor Maya Lin to put her signature on the building as well. Lin had achieved fame in the early 1980s with the Vietnam Memorial in Washington, D.C., where she cut contours in the earth to make a simple stone

Diagonals cut through the plaza directly to other buildings on the Principal campus. *Rainer Viertlboeck photograph. Courtesy of Jahn.*

Structural engineering elements are visible, and divisions between inside and out are largely transparent. *Rainer Viertlboeck photograph. Courtesy of Jahn.*

design unforgettable. At Principal, she asked herself, "Could I approach architecture the same way I approached the natural landscape?" Lin's intention was not to blend in with the architecture but rather to create a "work that physically would become part of the site." What she imagined was a wall that would dominate a three-level lobby, with water trickling slowly from end to end.

If Lin was not worried about how the architect would react to such a use of his space, Randy Manear was quite concerned. He was thinking that he was going to have to "referee" a battle between two strong-willed artists when the three of them met at Jahn's office on the edge of the Loop in Chicago. Manear knew that the German architect could be stubborn and resist even small changes in his design. Not this time. Jahn was pleased and supportive of the work, entitled *A Shift in the Stream*, an abstract work that became part of the building itself.

Chapter 12

DESIGNING DES MOINES' FUTURE

West Des Moines' West Valley Mall opened in 1971, which was not an architectural milestone except that one of its unintended consequences was an acceleration of the decline of downtown. Shoppers who once flocked to the Younkers and other stores in the compact commercial district between Fourth and Ninth Streets were getting on the interstates and going elsewhere.

Yet inherent pride in Des Moines prevented the decline from reaching the point of no return. That was proven when trucking magnate John Ruan built the thirty-four-story Ruan Center, completed in 1975. Set amid older buildings that were nostalgic and underperforming, the Ruan project was courageous as a real estate investment. It was also adventuresome in its architecture, clad in Cor-ten steel, which weathers to an intentionally oxidized patina. Ruan secured leases from major tenants such as Blue Cross Blue Shield and Banker's Trust, though the latter inspired one of the building's nicknames, "Bankers Rust."

Also in 1975, the Greater Des Moines Committee pushed for a new downtown auditorium. Civic leaders agreed that it was needed to replace the KRNT Theater, downtown's major performance venue, which was badly deteriorated. Optimistically, perhaps quixotically, the committee and the city commissioned a design for a full-blown convention center, including an auditorium, on a two-block site between Grand Avenue and Walnut Street. But then the bond referendum to pay for it failed, perhaps fortunately, as the project would have blocked the view down Locust Street to the Capitol. Whereupon, David Kreidenier and John Fitzgibbon—heads of the *Register* and the Iowa–Des Moines National Bank, respectively—embarked on a private fundraising effort, less than half the size of the referendum amount and outside the political line of fire. They succeeded and asked Charles E. Herbert and Associates to design what would be a $9 million auditorium and adjacent public space. It would become the Des Moines Civic Center and Nollen Plaza.

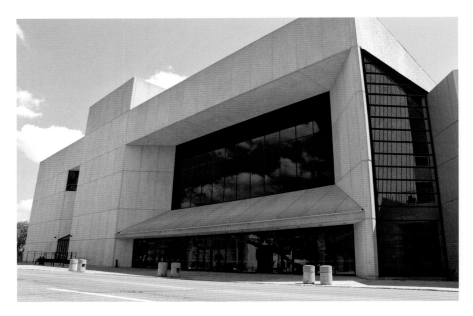

Des Moines Civic Center on the edge of downtown. *Courtesy of Des Moines Performing Arts.*

Charles "Chick" Herbert was an innovative, idealistic architect, but he was also adaptable. He was attuned to the latest building technologies and also highly collaborative with clients who were paying the bills, these being key assets for any successful architect. Born in Illinois, where his father owned a menswear store, Herbert graduated from Iowa State in architecture and engineering and soon married Adrienne Rickerd, a member of a well-connected Des Moines family. He enjoyed social relations with city's elite who were friends of his in-laws.

Herbert's interest in modern architecture also enabled him to assemble a firm of talented designers eager to try big things and get Des Moines to do them. So Herbert and company were ready when Kreidenier and Fitzgibbon approached Herbert about an auditorium. Perhaps the donors expected something glassy, but the architects recommended a different modern technology, not entirely new but very much on the modern cutting edge at the time. Construction for the new Civic Center (not to be confused with the civic center of the City Beautiful era) would be poured-in-place concrete. The style would be "Brutalism," a word that some, not all, found an apt description.

Brutalism was so named after Corbusier's *béton brut* or "raw concrete," and it had become an important approach to minimalist modernism at the time. In unskilled hands, the style could be harsh and even vulgar, but some of the twentieth century's great architects (Kahn, Nervi) achieved elegant form from lowly concrete. In Des Moines, I.M. Pei's Art Center wing of a few years before was widely praised. For the Civic Center, it was promising primarily because of cost; it could easily enclose a largely windowless performance space. Success depended on Herbert's manner of rendering it.

To achieve something sculptural, as explained by Herbert's associate (and later partner) Cal Lewis, the idea was to turn the building at a fifteen-degree angle to the street—this inspired by the the fact that downtown Des Moines' street grid is at a fifteen-degree angle to the overall "Jeffersonian" grid of the rest of the city and countryside. Amplifying this angle would bring a measure of geometric interest in what might have been a bland concrete box. The fifteen-degree (or greater) angle was repeated throughout the building, in its windows, doors and intersections of parts.

The building is simple, a credit to the firm whose mantra was "to do common things uncommonly well." Here it meant assembling the angles in an artistic way. "Chick always insisted that one big idea was usually enough," said another eventual Herbert partner, Kirk Blunck. This was essential advice, Blunck insisted, for many young architects with high ambition and too many ideas.

The practical simplicity of the design drove the interior as well. Continuous arcs of auditorium seats serve to push as much of the audience as visually close to the stage as possible. Its rake is lower than some theaters for acoustical reasons. "The whole design was a compromise between two requirements, music and theater," Lewis remembered. Its handsome simplicity proves that architects can

The interior of the Civic Center reflects the angular design applied outside. *Courtesy of Des Moines Performing Arts.*

achieve elegance without ornament, private boxes or any extra idea that would look excessive here.

While simple design has an enduring quality, time did take its toll, and thirty years on, renovations were overdue. David Kruidenier's nephew and ex-*Register* publisher Charles Edwards was recruited to lead fundraising, and he agreed to get involved only if the upgrades to the auditorium were accompanied by a major renovation of Nollen Plaza. After a hiatus due to the 2008 recession, the indoor-outdoor project moved ahead. New York–based landscape designer Ken Smith, a native Iowan, was brought in to transform the urban park between the Civic Center and Capitol Square. Smith angled a walk through the space at the customary fifteen-degree angle and on axis with the auditorium. A light sculpture by artist Jim Campbell joined the Claus Oldenberg piece already there. Cowles Commons, as it is now called, connects the Civic Center with the rest of the city in a more navigable manner than before. It also connects the design approach of the 1970s with that of the twenty-first century, simply and without a clash of spirit or style.

PRACTICAL URBAN PLANNING

The Civic Center was, and remains, a success story. But even when it was new, there was a feeling that restoring the city's vitality required something more than individual projects. In the early 1970s, one active debate hinged on parking and whether garages should be underground or above. Above was the expedient choice, and this led to one of the city's early Skywalks, between the Grand Avenue Garage and the Ruan Center. Its perceived success motivated the city to expand the Skywalk system throughout downtown. Proponents, including Mayor Richard Olson, believed it was essential to keep downtown office buildings populated; architects surrendered to it as a "necessary evil."

It fell to an outsider to make a decisive move for truly efficacious planning to move Des Moines ahead. Mario Gandelsonas, urbanist and architect then at Yale's School of Architecture, taught a seminar on urbanism, and he was looking for a real-life laboratory, a city, to apply advanced ideas. Chicago architect Bruce Graham of Skidmore Owings and Merrill (recent Capital Square architects) told him that Des Moines had many qualities that Gandelsonas had long cited as prerequisites to good urban planning. It was small. It had rivers running through it. And it had a well-educated populace.

Gandelsonas's approach to cities was different from that of most others at the time. Modernist urban planning tended to superimpose ideal features on a map that, if built, would lead to a happy and healthy result. Understanding that such initiatives rarely worked very well, Gandelsonas approached the process more holistically by understanding what already existed in a city and amplifying positive features. This often required looking beneath the surface. "I wanted to teach students how to *read* the city, how to get to know it intimately," Gandelsonas said.

What impressed Gandelsonas most about Des Moines was the downtown grid, turned at that fifteen-degree angle to the rest of the city. He also noted that the two streets that cut through at the angle, Grand and Locust, constituted a corridor in which much of the city's activity was concentrated. "I was fascinated by this," he said. "It was as if an architect had designed it."

Yet accessing this corridor was not always easy, Gandelsonas said, or at least it was unlovely. He was outraged by the drive from Des Moines' "international airport," as he called it, which passed through several blocks of tire stores and lube shops before a driver could get downtown. It led him to the logical notion that entries or "gateways" to downtown Des Moines needed to be enhanced. That led, after at least a decade of effort, to the creation of the Western Gateway Park and within it the Pappajohn Sculpture Park.

Some of Gandelsonas's writings are dense and theoretical, but his methods are clear and ultimately extremely patient. And as he and his students "de-layered" the city to understand its physical and social makeup, he devised savvy strategies to realize a park. Early on he allied himself with Chick Herbert and other business leaders. A shared vision for a Gateway Park developed, so strong that when the city council said that it could afford a one-block park and nothing larger, a downtown alliance responded. It said that the opposite was true, that Des Moines could not afford a one-block park because businesses wouldn't support it. They would, however, raise funds for a five-block gateway. As money was cobbled together, most from private sources, acquisition of buildings and teardowns began by the mid-'90s.

MEREDITH'S DOWNTOWN HEADQUARTERS

Meredith Corporation, with its headquarters on the western edge of the Gateway property, became an early powerful supporter of the plan. The publishing company already had a history of supporting downtown; in the 1980s, it had hired the Herbert firm to preserve part of its 1912 headquarters in a thorough modernization of that building—this as opposed to leaving the city for the suburbs, as had been contemplated. Blending old structures with new ones was rarely done at the time, and the idea of architectural preservation was still vague. But the concept succeeded, saving the façade and tower originally designed by Proudfoot and Bird. This project, led by the Hebert firm's Cal Lewis, was praised in *Time* magazine.

Above: The most striking renaissance in the Gateway Park, and Meredith's part in it, came at night. *Farshid Assassi photograph. Courtesy of HLKB and Knowles Blunck Architecture.*

Left: The new modern architecture in Meredith emphasizes connections between floors and from outside to in. *Farshid Assassi photograph. Courtesy of HLKB and Knowles Blunck Architecture.*

More than a decade later, the company would advance the Gandelsonas idea with new buildings that would serve as a sort of portal to the Gateway Park. "One of the things that we were taught in school was that buildings shape interior spaces and exterior space," said Paul Mankins, then a young architect with the Herbert firm. For a new and much expanded Meredith headquarters, HLKB won the commission and created an imposing L-shaped headquarters with a squared-off "arch" over Locust Street. It created something of a piazza (with a campanile, the old tower) through which people would pass before they entered the park.

Just as the brutalist Civic Center was appropriate for its time and place, the Meredith expansion was equally well suited to its use. Steel frames and glass walls provide a transparency (a common corporate ideal) and reinforce the idea that the building is part of a series of overlapping public and private places. Its relatively narrow footprint enables abundant natural light. Inside, its glassiness and balconies encourage visual contact among employees. As a 2001 book on HLKB explains, the building is a series of "agoras capable of keeping up with the rhythm and pace of American cities." The American Institute of Architects (AIA) gave the project a national honor award. "The interaction between site and building, existing and new, large and small, landscape and structure, combine to assemble a convincingly orchestrated total," the AIA said in its citation.

BOOKEND AND A STRIKING NEW LIBRARY

As the Meredith building was being constructed, plans were underway for other elements of the park, including a new Central Library, the other "bookend" of the Western Gateway. With the new century approaching, the community agreed that a modern building was needed to replace the Des Moines Library that had been in use since 1903. A committee of citizens and government officials, along with librarians, believed that such a project would not only enhance the park, but it was also an opportunity to bring to Des Moines a new building of international repute.

Big-name architects were willing, and among finalists who made public presentations in Des Moines were Gwathmey Segal, Michael Graves, Will Bruder and David Chipperfield. As the committee narrowed the field, some favored Bruder because his focus was on a library that would serve children and underprivileged populations. Members of the philanthropic community were more attracted by Chipperfield, and particularly his understanding of the Western Gateway. In Chipperfield's initial schemes, the building's footprint was irregular and even curvilinear, promising that such a library, if built, would create unique spaces inside and out.

The Des Moines Public Library's copper-infused glass walls are both simple and striking. *Farshid Assassi photograph. Courtesy of David Chipperfield Architects and Des Moines Public Library.*

The library's green roof on the edge of the Western Gateway. *Farshid Assassi photograph. Courtesy of David Chipperfield Architects and Des Moines Public Library.*

Architect Chipperfield, of London, was working at that very time on the Figge Museum of Art in Davenport and had joined on that project with HLKB to carry out the design of the building. The same relationship was forged for Des Moines, and while HLKB downplayed its role in the design, the local firm was critical in mediating elements that were demanded by the community. One was a green roof, which was suggested when occupants of office buildings nearby expressed discomfort in staring down on machinery and gravel. Plantings on the roof became part of a broader sustainable design already recognized as a keynote of contemporary architecture.

Chipperfield and HLKB were well suited as partners, if only because both were known for taking simplicity to a reasonable extreme. As the $25 million budget was hardly luxurious, the final building was a simplified version of the original scheme, but it accomplished many of the same things. Large open spaces provided for book stacks. The irregular shape provided for nooks and crannies for readers and courtyards outside. The basic concrete structure would absorb heat and cool and stabilize temperatures. What was not basic nor inexpensive was the copper-colored window walls of the building's exterior. It was made from copper mesh within two layers of glass, an effective device to shade the interior from intense sun. Of course, it was the aesthetics of the curtain wall that dazzled. In the daytime, it is rich in color and vaguely translucent. It becomes transparent when the lights are on at night. "At sunset," said Paul Mankins who worked on the project for HLKB, "it dematerializes."

MODERN TEMPLE OF PRESERVATION

In the evolution of Chipperfield's idea, the library might have been separate from other buildings, with a grove of trees on one end and pushed up against older parts of the city on the other. There were impulses even to raze the Masonic Temple, just east, except that the better lights of preservation were active as well as the Western Gateway developed. Ultimately, library and temple became harmonious neighbors, with an intimate, well-used courtyard between. It required steady coordination between the owner of the old building and architect of the new to achieve that result.

The couple who were restoring the old building, Pamela and Harry Bookey, came with equal passion for their building and plan to create in it a performing arts center. Pamela had been chairman of the Greater Des Moines Public Art Foundation. Harry is a real estate developer with a national portfolio. In 1999, when demolition of older buildings began to clear the Western Gateway, the Bookeys looked beneath the shabby exterior of the Masonic Temple, a 1913 Neoclassical work of Proudfoot, Bird and Rawson. By this time, it had precarious tenants, such as Alcoholics Anonymous, a massage therapist and a wig shop.

The Bookeys imagined income-producing stores and offices to support a place otherwise dedicated to music and theater. The idea sometimes seemed starry-eyed in the extreme. It needed a restaurant for income, but operators who looked at it said that it would be hard to get people to come to this part of town at night. Exactly,

The old Masonic Temple is now the Temple for the Performing Arts. *Ben Easter photograph. Courtesy of the photographer.*

A room designed for Masonic rituals is now a recital hall. *Ben Easter photograph. Courtesy of the photographer.*

said the Bookeys, who eventually became partners themselves in the Italian restaurant Centro. They also enlisted the help of Iowa's Governor Vilsack to cajole Starbucks to locate there—largely overcoming the company's policy not to open in unredeveloped downtowns. Upstairs there were surer assets where the Proudfoot firm had applied customary skill in creating a Grand Hall with a colonnade and stained-glass skylight, suitable for banquets. Also crucial, the Des Moines Symphony took offices and studios in the building.

Opening in 2002, the Temple for the Performing Arts was successful enough to nearly break even after a decade. It certainly changed the music landscape in Des Moines, and perhaps just as important, it became an object lesson for preservationists of the future. It was an unlikely project that succeeded for dozens of small reasons, many of which the owners themselves undertook on a hands-on basis. They mediated with neighbors (such as the library) and made allies of potential antagonists. They fought the city to allow them sidewalk seating for the restaurant. They kept track of the caterers who handled the banquet hall and finally found the right one. The Bookeys even got involved in calculating savings by changing light bulbs, thousands per year, yet another one of the incremental line items that enabled the Bookeys to break even.

THE PAPPAJOHN EFFECT

When the Western Gateway became open space, it was a start, but that alone was not transformative. The city would have to "improve" the area around it with projects that would infuse the park with life. Its future depended on the ability of investors and their architects to transform the Gateway not just physically also but culturally.

Educational needs became a natural part of the conversation and inspired the idea that Iowa colleges and universities might share a building in Des Moines for continuing and adult education programs. Civic leader John Pappajohn became a ready donor for this project, which initially involved seven institutions of higher education, including the three major state universities. Nothing like it had been done before, and perhaps predictably the consortium encountered stormy waters in keeping the institutions lined up and in agreement. Yet Pappajohn, a wealthy entrepreneur who understands the power of collaboration, provided the determined force necessary to realize a building with a function that could transform a part of the Gateway Park.

The architectural challenge of the John and Mary Pappajohn Education Center, eventually operated by the University of Iowa, was to help populate the park while keeping precious open space as open as possible. In the design, HLKB used the same basic strategy as in Meredith: transparent glass walls to make the building less a barrier and more a part of the larger space around it. It made use of the latest technologies at

John and Mary Pappajohn Education Center on the edge of Western Gateway Park. *Courtesy of HLKB and Knowles Blunck Architecture.*

the time, such as fritted glass (with patterns stamped on the surface) to provide shade without impeding views, also older ones such as Cor-ten steel louvers. The effect is that the Pappajohn Center's walls aren't so much walls as they are screens, appropriate if not symbolic for an open interior equipped with digital learning equipment.

Shortly after the building named for him opened in 2005, John Pappajohn drove by and was struck by a new thought: that the Gateway Park, which was manicured but mostly empty, could be a place for his major collection of contemporary sculpture. He quickly called a member of the city council, Christine Hensley, who agreed that it would be excellent to donate some fifteen outdoor sculptures to be installed in a portion of what was now public land.

So did Jeff Fleming, director of the Des Moines Arts Center, though as the idea developed, they agreed that the full city block envisioned would need more than fifteen sculptures to fill it out. Fleming later said that carrying it through was a sign of Pappajohn's implacable commitment to Des Moines' improvement and also of the city's progressive spirit that it would embark on a project to reconfigure a park that had so recently been cleared and landscaped. The project grew to feature twenty-one works by international artists, including Willem deKooning, Martin Puryear, Keith Haring and Jaume Plensa, among others. The pieces of sculpture, all selected by Pappajohn—already an important American collector—made emphatic statements. Plensa's *Nomade* has become an iconic image with its form of a giant human head

Transparency and connectivity mark the Pappajohn Center. *Ben Easter photograph. Courtesy of the photographer.*

The learning mission of the Pappajohn Center was designed into the building's optics and infrastructure. *Courtesy of HLKB and Knowles Blunck Architecture.*

The John and Mary Pappajohn Sculpture Park, centerpiece of the Gateway and noted worldwide for its public art. *Courtesy of Des Moines Art Center.*

In a renovation of a 1970s house designed by sustainability pioneer Ray Crites, HLKB discovered what ties the twenty-first century to mid-century modern. *Courtesy of HLKB and Knowles Blunck Architecture.*

shaped from letters of the alphabet. Architects particularly approve of *T8* by Mark di Severo, who was a construction worker before he became an artist famous for compositions of structural steel.

The John and Mary Pappajohn Sculpture Park "showed how art has the ability to change the landscape, not just culturally but economically as well," said Fleming. He means that it became a direct catalyst to development in the area. Blue Cross Blue Shield built a headquarters that amplifies the park's open space with a semicircular plaza on its site across Grand Avenue from the park. Nationwide Insurance occupies the other side with a modern building that lines the street. The quality of the sculpture, as well as the quality of new buildings around it, is comparable to other such projects in Chicago and Minneapolis. Few projects like this one have so emphatically transformed the area around it.

THE CURVE OF THE NEW CENTURY

Architectural traditions in Des Moines reveal themselves in many ways, including in the long lives of important firms. As we've seen, Proudfoot and Bird has changed names a number of time over the decades, settling in recent years with the name Brooks, Borg and Skiles. The firm has made its mark on Des Moines in several modern downtown buildings such as the glassy Convention Center, now the new YMCA, and most recently the EMC Building, a twenty-story vaguely postmodern high-rise. What is most advanced about the latter building is a German-designed "rainscreen," a layered curtainwall system that keeps moisture from condensing on the building's exterior and results in energy savings.

Also significant was the trajectory of HLKB. With five partners by the turn of the twenty-first century, the firm continued in a range of work, including interiors and even parking ramps. HLKB also widened the preservation movement, significantly when Kirk Blunck led the office in a renovation called the Moen House, a residence originally designed by architect Ray Crites. Crites was a pioneer in sustainable architecture and influential in the 1970s. After two decades it needed work, and though mid-century modern architecture would become an important focus of architectural preservation in time, it had few proponents in the year 2000.

The Moen project illustrates how architecture of the twenty-first century has returned to the simplicity of the '70s. In a portfolio that extended throughout Iowa, Crites often used reinforced concrete for its economic and heat-absorbing qualities. He also experimented with solar collectors, and he embedded some houses in the earth. As a professor at Iowa State in the 1970s, he introduced a generation of young architects (including Rod Kruse, later of HLKB) to what would be called "green architecture."

Blunck's approach to the Moen House was primarily to restore an openness to an interior that had been broken up into smaller spaces shortly after it was built. He restored, for example, its lateral axis and long sight lines on each of two floors. Some things have been changed, such as finishes in more luxurious materials than Crites

In the Moen House's updating, the lines of 1960s retro-style furniture appear entirely up to date. *Courtesy of HLKB and Knowles Blunck Architecture.*

would have used. Yet black-stained ash, polished granite and limestone and stainless steel, which are striking and (arguably) organic, are not radically different in spirit from the equally striking board-form concrete and earthen roof of the original.

HLKB dissolved in 2011. (Chick Herbert died in 2010.) At least two successor firms have endeavored to carry on its spirit with projects that are sometmes modest but

The Principal Riverwalk Pavilion, otherwise known as the Hub Stop. *Paul Crosby photograph.*

DART central transit station slopes from a mostly vacant industrial district and upward toward the high-rises of downtown. *Ben Easter photograph. Courtesy of the photographer.*

usually progressive. Among those firms, Substance Architecture, started by ex-HLKB partner Paul Mankins, designed a small but conspicuous landmark, the Principal Riverwalk Pavilion, or "Hub Spot," a café and rest stop. Paired with another sculptural building, the Riverwalk Pump Station, they constitute a substantial updating of the downtown riverfront.

The designs of these buildings show how creative solutions can be applied to small projects. The Hub Spot is glassy and angular; it sits atop the embankment and on a barely perceptible upward slope, a device that enables people sitting on the café terrace to see over the essential parapet of the flood wall. The Pump Station, with equipment to curtail flooding during high water, might otherwise be a cinder block container. But almost adjacent to the cheerful Hub Spot, the two make similar but different uses of the same palette. The Pump Station, with opaque glass and horizontal stripes of color, explains Substance partner Tim Hickman, offsets the café's transparent walls and colorful columns outside.

Substance also brought high design to a normally utilitarian type of building in the DART bus station, a few steps from the Polk County Courthouse. If this was not an unlikely project for advanced architecture, it was an unlikely site: a wedge of property just south of downtown. Here, the wedge became a leitmotif for an otherwise simple glass and zinc-sheet building. With the wedge (subtly) in mind, the glass box is amplified with an array of diagonal lines, such as the shed pitched roof over the main building and cable stays that hold a canopy over transfer platforms. The intention was to incorporate crucial values of twenty-first-century architecture—simplicity, sustainability and elegant use of economical materials.

Yet another thoroughly modern public building went up in 2011 in the shadow of the State Capitol, for the Iowa Utilities Board and the Office of Consumer Advocate. It is a building of admirable clarity, made mostly of zinc cladding and glass. Metal louvers in front of south-facing windows emphasize what is true in invisible elements as well—that this building is an energy-saving machine. The clarity of that design began, said Rod Kruse, a principal of the firm BNIM that designed it, with an ultra-clear objective.

The Utilities Board (which shares space with the Iowa Consumer Advocate) acts as the state's regulator of utilities, so it was natural when new space was needed that it serve as a demonstration project for sustainability. Ambitiously, the board presented the architects with goals for energy consumption amounting to energy consumption at least 50 percent under that of older buildings. It then supported a design process that proposed and measured projected results.

The building began with its siting to take advantage of passive solar heat. It maximizes natural sunlight and ventilation due to the building's layout with wings that are narrow enough for all parts of the interior to be close to outside walls. On a more advanced level, the building is built to benefit from photovoltaic cells applied to the exterior. Even metal louvers on south-facing windows were set at an angle determined by computer modeling to maximize light, especially in winter, and also moderate summer heat. While these were hardly groundbreaking strategies, what made this project successful, said project architect Carey Nagle, was their assembly. Nagle talks about avoiding "thermal bridges," where heat or cold is conducted and reduce energy

The environmental approach to the Iowa Utilities Board building involves computer-modeled sunshades and extends to the restored prairies nearby. *Farshid Assassi photograph. Courtesy of BNIM.*

The interior of Iowa Utilities Board shows how sustainability has become fashionable. *Mike Sinclair photograph. Courtesy of BNIM.*

The Iowa Utilities Board building with view of the Capitol. *Mike Sinclair photograph. Courtesy of BNIM.*

efficiency. They are eliminated not just by knowledge and use of innovative materials, but also through care in construction—such as that achieved by modernists who built sixty and seventy years ago.

The Utilities Board building represents encouraging trends for many reasons. One is that it responds to compelling social need; it is admirable for the strides that it makes in sheer sustainability. But it has particular resonance in Iowa as well, because its beauty is also wrought of precision in engineering and construction. That harks to some of the more important buildings of Des Moines' past, such as those of Saarinen and Mies, who found such a hospitable climate in Des Moines for their architecture, which has truly stood the test of time.

SELECT BIBLIOGRAPHY

M ost of these books, articles and reports deal directly or indirectly with specific aspects of Des Moines architecture.

BOOKS

Gebhard, David, and Gerald Mansheim. *Buildings of Iowa* (Buildings of the United States Series). New York: Oxford University Press, 1993.

Goettsch, Scherrie, and Steve Weinberg. *Terrace Hill: The Story of a House and the People Who Touched It.* Des Moines, IA: Wallace-Homestead Book Co., 1979.

Hitchcock, Henry-Russell, and William Seale. *Temples of Democracy: The State Capitols of the U.S.A.* New York: Harcourt Brace Jovanovich, 1976.

Johnson, Linda Nelson, Jerry C. Miller and Jesse Masciangelo. *The Iowa Capitol: A Harvest of Design.* Des Moines, IA: Plain Talk Publishing, 1989.

Kuhn, Nicola, and Helmut Jahn. *Archi-Neering: Helmut Jahn, Werner Sobek.* Ostfildern, Germany: Hatje Cantz Verlag, 2000.

Lyons, Maura. *Building a Modern Campus: Eliel and Eero Saarinen at Drake University.* Published by Drake University to accompany an exhibit of the same title. Des Moines, IA: Drake University, 2008.

Noun, Louise Rosenfeld, et al. *An Uncommon Vision: The Des Moines Art Center.* New York: Hudson Hills, 1998.

Pease, George Sexton. *Patriarch of the Prairie: The Story of Equitable of Iowa, 1867–1967.* New York: Appleton-Century-Crofts, 1967.

Pelkonen, Eeva-Liisa. *Eero Saarinen: Shaping the Future.* New Haven, CT: Yale University Press, 2006.

Román, Antonio. *Eero Saarinen: An Architecture of Multiplicity.* New York: Princeton Architectural Press, 2003.

Saarinen, Eliel. *The City: Its Growth, Its Decay, Its Future.* New York: Reinhold Publishing, 1943.

Sadowsky, Laura M. *Salisbury House.* Des Moines, IA: Salisbury House Foundation, 2015.

Shank, Wesley. *Iowa's Historic Architects.* Iowa City: University of Iowa Press, 1998.

Wilson, Richard Guy, and Sidney K. Robinson. *The Prairie School in Iowa.* Ames: Iowa State University Press, 1987.

ARTICLES

In the *Annals of Iowa*, published by the State Historical Society of Iowa since 1863, articles pertinent to Des Moines architecture include:

Dey, Peter A. "Recollections of the Old Capitol and the New." 1905.
Ferraro, William M. "Representing a Layered Community: James, Lampson P., and Hoyt Sherman and the Development of Des Moines, 1850–1900." Summer 1998.
Kasson, John A. "The Fight for the New Capitol." 1900.
Thomson, Linda K. "Terrace Hill: A Magnificent Gift to the State of Iowa." Spring 1972.
Wagner, William. "William Foster: Early Iowa Architect." Summer 1962.

OTHER ARTICLES OF HISTORICAL INTEREST

Alread, Jason, and Thomas Leslie. "A Museum of Living Architecture: Continuity and Contradiction at the Des Moines Art Center." *Journal of Architectural Education*, November, 2007.
MacVicar, John. "The Des Moines Municipal Building." *The American City*, 1912.
Robinson, Charles Mulford. "Improvement in City Life: Aesthetic Progress." *Atlantic Monthly*, June 1899.
"Total Design on a Grand Scale" (about Eero Saarinen's CBS Building in Manhattan and SOM's American Republic Building in Des Moines). *Life* magazine, April 29, 1966.
Whitehead, Robert. "Tectonics, Tolerances, and Time: Examining Eero Saarinen's and Mies van der Rohe's Buildings at Drake University, Des Moines, Iowa." *Preservation Education and Research* 2 (2009).
Zeller, John. "From the Real to the Ideal: Images of Des Moines in the Pregressive Era," article accompanies website Historic Des Moines: Images of Des Moines, 1904–1914 created by Cowles Library, Drake University.

UNPUBLISHED REPORTS

Among many papers produced in the interests of preservations, especially for the National Register of Historic Places, these reports are available at the Research Center of the State Historical Society of Iowa.

Eckhardt, Patricia. "Des Moines' Commercial Architecture, 1876–1937: An Historic Context and Survey of Sites," prepared for the Planning and Zoning Department, City of Des Moines, 1995.
Long, Barbara Beving. "The Architectural Legacy of Proudfoot & Bird in Iowa, 1882–1940," written to support the inclusion of buildings by Proudfoot and Bird buildings in the National Register of Historic Places, 1988.
Mohr, Paula H. "Salisbury House," written to amend the inclusion of Salisbury House in the National Register of Historic Places, 2005.

INDEX

A

Aldrich, Charles 35
Allée 125, 126
Allen, Benjamin Franklin 9, 13, 15, 17, 18, 22, 37, 38, 39, 65
American Foursquare 43
American Gothic 61
American Male 137
American Republic insurance building 134, 137
American Society of Landscape Architects 142
Architectural Forum 111
Architectural Record 132
Armand Company 71, 72, 75
Art Deco 76, 95, 100, 101, 131, 132, 133, 138
Art Nouveau 59
Arts and Crafts 18, 52, 59, 70, 110, 119
AT&T Tower 138

B

Bacon, Francis 117
Banker's Life Building (Corporate One) 11, 131, 132, 134
Barber, George F. 67, 68
Bartlett, Benjamin J. 42
Beaux-Arts style 33, 84, 85, 86, 91, 96, 100
Bedford limestone 85
Bennett Boyd, Byron 72
Berlage, Hendrik Petrus 129
Bird, George W. 86, 95, 96, 98, 149
Blashfield, Edwin 30
Blunck, Kirk 11, 56, 147, 160
Bookey, Pamela and Harry 153, 155
Boyd and Moore 71
Boyington, William 15, 16, 17
Brazil, Father John 61
Bridal Row 41, 42
Brooks, Borg and Skiles 95, 98, 160
Brooks, John 110
Brown, Talmadge E. 43
Brutalism 111, 146
Bunshaft, Gordon 135, 137

Burnham, Daniel 52, 98
Bussard Dikis 32
Butler Mansion 76, 77, 114

C

Capitol Square 148
Carnegie, Andrew 85
Carpenter's Gothic style 38, 41
Casavant organ 61
Centro 155
Chateauesque style 69, 70
Chicago 9, 13, 15, 16, 17, 25, 26, 33, 52,
        61, 81, 82, 86, 98, 99, 100, 129, 142,
        144, 148, 160
Chicago School 52, 98
Chipperfield, David 11, 151, 152, 153
Chrysler Building 142
City Beautiful movement 80, 81, 82, 91,
        93, 146
Cochrane, John 25, 26
Coggeshall, Mary 93
Connecticut General Insurance 135
Corbusier 76, 113, 135, 146
Court Avenue 47, 49
Cowles Commons 148
Craftsman 43
Cranbrook School 110, 119
Crawford House 69, 70, 72
Crites, Ray 160
Cubist style 124, 126, 129

D

DART bus station 162, 163
Davis, Stuart 125, 126
deKooning, Willem 156
Des Moines arsenal 83
Des Moines Building 95, 96, 100, 101, 132
Des Moines Civic Center 11, 83, 145

Des Moines Fine Arts Association 107
Des Moines Fire Department
        Headquarters 104
Des Moines Plan 91, 93, 94
Des Moines Public Library 33, 81, 152
Des Moines River 80, 82, 84
Des Moines Saddlery 47, 48, 49
Des Moines Social Club 105
Des Moines Women's Club 81, 107
de Stijl movement 129
Dikis, Bill 32
Disciples of Christ 127
Drake University 75, 118, 119

E

Edmundson, James D. 107, 109
Egan, James 61, 62
801 Grand Avenue 138, 139
EMC Building 160
Equitable Building 95, 96, 98, 99, 132, 141
Ericsson, Larry 21

F

Fenton, Scotney 32
Ferraro, William M. 38
Figge Museum of Art 152
Fitch Hall of Pharmacy 120, 121
Fitzgibbon, John 145, 146
Fleming Building 52, 54, 98
Fleming, Jeff 156, 159
Foster and Liebbe 57, 65, 95
Foster, William 65
French Second Empire style 14, 15, 24, 25, 37

G

Galveston Plan 93
Gandelsonas, Mario 11, 148, 149, 151

General Motors Technical Center (Bloomfield Hills, Michigan) 119

Georgian style 118, 132

Gilded Age 24, 30, 37, 39, 70, 90

Giralda Tower 86

Goldman, Harold 79

Gothic Revival 16, 40, 45, 57, 59, 65, 98

GQ magazine 142

Great Depression 76, 100, 107

green men (grotesques) 87, 91

Greenwood Park 10, 109, 110, 112, 118

Gross, Marty 44

Gross, Ralph 44

Gugler, Eric 110

Gutterson, Frank 33, 84, 85

H

Hallett, George 100

Haring, Keith 156

Harmon, Henry G. 118, 119, 123

Hatch, Representative Jack G. 45

Hellmuth, Obata and Kassabaum (HOK) 138

Hensley, Christine 156

Herbert, Charles E. "Chick" 11, 12, 145, 146, 147, 149, 151, 161

Herndon Hall 65, 66, 67, 69

Hickman, Tim 163

Hippee Building 54

Hirsch, Dr. Norma 44

Historical, Memorial and Art Building (now the Ola Babcock Miller Building) 33

Hoffman, William E. 49

Home Federal Savings and Loan 64

Homestead Building 49, 50

Hopper, Edward 117

Houser, Lowell 133

Hubbell Building 54, 95, 98

Hubbell Dining Hall 124, 125

Hubbell, Frederick Marion 17, 18, 19, 22, 67

Hub Spot 162, 163

Hunter, Jeff and Janet 68

Hunt, Richard Morris 24

Huttenlocher, Christopher 67, 68

I

Icanrians 25

Ingham Hall of Science 120

Iowa–Des Moines National Bank 101, 132, 145

Iowa Utilities Board and the Office of Consumer Advocate Building 163, 164

Italianate style 39, 40, 47, 48, 49

J

Jahn, Helmut 142, 144

Jefferson, Thomas 119

John and Mary Pappajohn Education Center 155, 156

John and Mary Pappajohn Sculpture Park 158, 159

Johnson, Philip 119, 128, 138

K

Kahn, Louis 128, 146

Kasson, John A. 23, 24

Kettle River sandstone 85

King's House (Salisbury) 71, 75

knapped flint masonry 73, 75

Kraetsch and Kraetsch 76

Kreidenier, David 145, 146

Kruse, Rod 160, 163

L

Lannon limestone 110

Le Grand, Iowa limestone 35

Lever House (New York) 135
Lewis, Cal 147, 149
Lin, Maya 142, 144
Linton, Shauneen 45
Lyons, Maura 118, 119

M

Madison Square Garden (New York) 86
Mahaska County 107
Maish House 39, 40, 44
Manear, Randy 142, 144
Mankins, Paul 128, 151, 153, 162
Manning, Warren H. 82
Marquardt and Wetherell 21
Masonic Temple 153, 154
McCammon, Rob 46
McCaw, Dr. John 10, 127, 128
McClure, Judy 45
McKim, Mead and White 24, 70
Medbury Hall 126, 127
Meier, Richard 113, 114, 115, 117
Meredith Corporation 11, 149
Meredith Hall 64, 129, 130
Mies van der Rohe, Ludwig 10, 11, 64, 76, 128, 129, 130, 166
Moen House 160
Moore, Herbert 72
Moraine, Tim 33
Mullins, Reginald 72
Municipal Building 9, 10, 80, 92, 93, 94

N

Nagle, Carey 163
National Gallery (Washington) 109, 111
Neutra, Richard 79

New York Five 113, 117
Nollen, Gerard 131
Nollen Plaza 145, 148

O

Obata, Gyo 138, 140
Oldenberg, Claus 148
old post office 80
One Liberty Place (Philadelphia) 142
Oreon E. Scott Chapel 10, 126
Owl's Head 68, 132

P

Panama-Pacific Exposition 107
Pappajohn, John 155, 156
Pei, I.M. 111, 113, 114, 146
Pella, Iowa 131
Piety Hill 57, 59, 61, 72
Piquenard, Alfred H. 25, 26
Plensa, Jaume 156
Polk County Courthouse 95, 98, 163
Pope, John Russell 109
Porter, Jack 42, 43
postmodernism 114, 138, 140, 142
Powell, Watson, Jr. 134, 135, 137, 138
Powell, Watson, Sr. 137
Principal Financial 11, 131, 138, 139
Principal Riverwalk 12, 162
Pritzker Prize 114
Progressive Architecture 123
Progressive Era 92
Proudfoot and Bird 11, 76, 85, 86, 93, 95, 96, 98, 149, 160
Proudfoot, Bird and Rawson 54, 72, 95, 98, 153

Proudfoot, William 86, 95
Puryear, Martin 156

Q

Quadrangle Dormitories 124, 126
Queen Anne style 40, 41, 66, 67

R

Raccoon River 13
Rasmussen, William Whitney 72
Rawson, Harry 100, 101
Ray, Governor Robert E. 21
Redhead, Wesley 38
Renaissance Design Group 32
Richardson, H.H. 24, 49, 69
Richardsonian Romanesque 49, 62, 69, 70,
    84, 96
Rickerd, Adrienne 146
Riverwalk Pump Station 162
Roberts, Thomas A. 65
Robinson, Charles Mumford 82
Root, John Wellborn 62
Ruan Center 145, 148
Ruan, John 145
Rubelman, Jacob 47
Rudolph, Paul 128

S

Saarinen, Eero 10, 11
Sacred Heart Cathedral (Davenport) 62
Salisbury, England 71, 72, 73
Sanford, Arthur 100, 101
Schinkel, Karl Friedrich 129
Schlarmann, David 45
Scott, Willson Alexander 22
Shank, Wesley 86, 92

Sherman Hill 37, 39, 41, 42, 43, 44, 45, 46,
    66, 68
Sherman Hill Association 44, 45
Sherman, Hoyt 42
Sheuerman House 41, 44, 45
Shift in the Stream, A 144
Sixth Avenue Canyon 100, 101, 140
Skidmore Owings and Merrill 134, 148
Skywalk 138, 148
Slingshot 105
Smith and Gutterson 33, 84
Smith, Ken 148
Smith, Oliver 33, 50
Smithsonian Institution 109, 110
St. Ambrose Cathedral 61, 62, 64
Strauss, Benjamin 43
St. Thomas Aquinas 129
Sullivan, Louis 62, 141

T

Taenzer, York 44, 45
Taylor, James Knox 91
Teachout, Horace 54
Temple for the Performing Arts 154, 155
Terrace Hill 9, 13, 15, 17, 18, 19, 21, 24,
    37, 38, 65, 67, 109, 132
Terrace Hill Society 21
Time magazine 149
Tribune Tower Competition 99
Trier House 10, 78
Tudor Revival style 74, 78

U

Upjohn, Richard 57, 61

V

Van Buren County 26

W

Wagner, William 19
Walker, Peter 142
Warhol, Andy 134, 137, 138
Weeks, Carl 71, 72, 73, 75
Western Gateway Park 11, 149, 156
West Valley Mall 145
Westward 30, 32
WHO radio 131
Wood, Grant 61, 133
World's Columbian Exposition 33, 52, 81
Wright, Frank Lloyd 10, 17, 43, 78, 79,
        100, 110
Wrigley Building (Chicago) 86

Z

Z Building (Corporate Four) 141, 142

ABOUT THE AUTHOR

Jay Pridmore's background as a Chicago journalist has sharpened and informed his impassioned study of architectural history. He is the author of over twenty books, including *Chicago Architecture and Design*, *University of Chicago: The Campus Guide*, *Shanghai: The Architecture of China's Great Urban Center* and *The American Bicycle*.

Visit us at
www.historypress.net
....
This title is also available as an e-book